AF371817

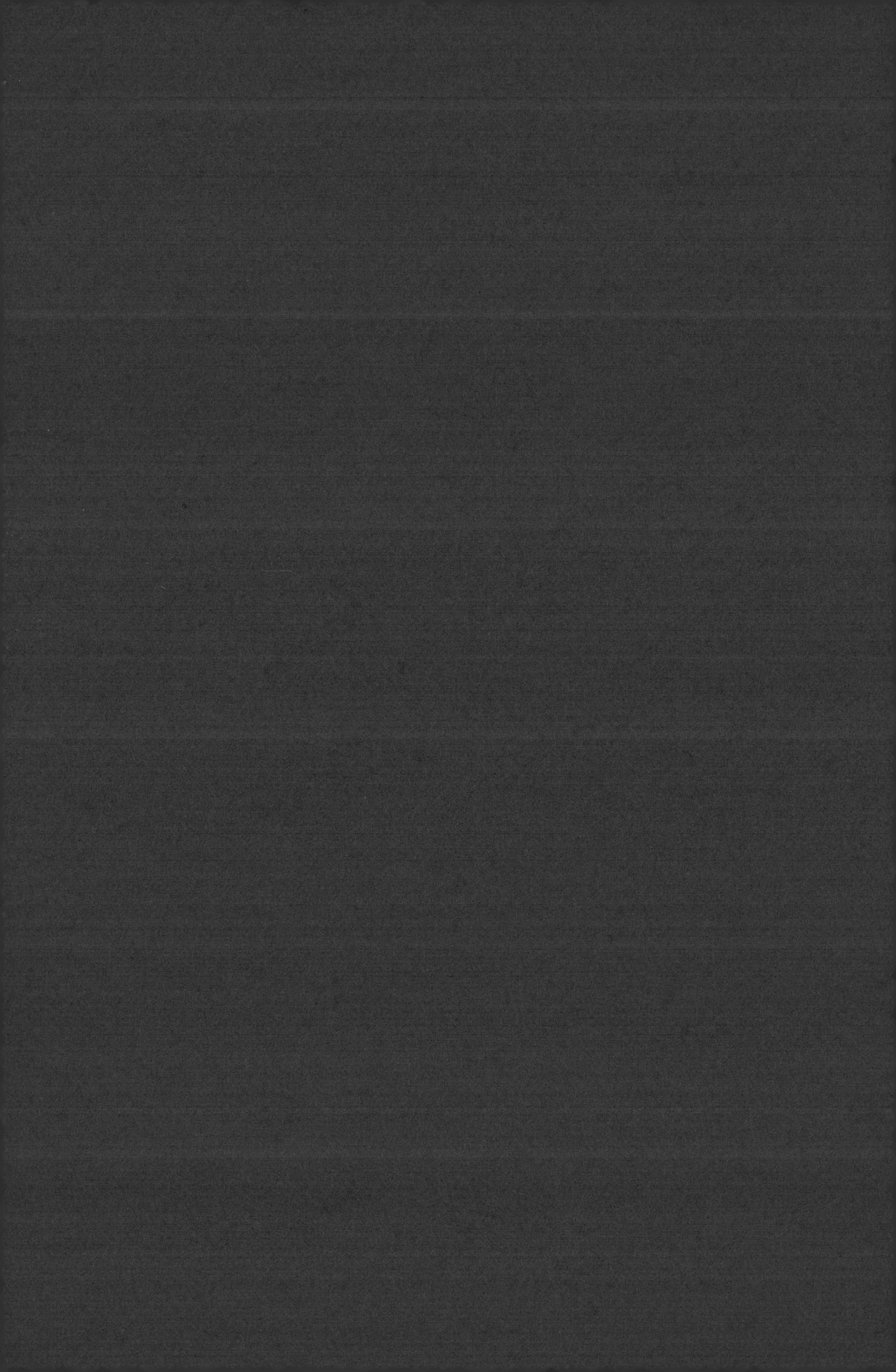

Haegue Yang
Flat Works

SKIRA

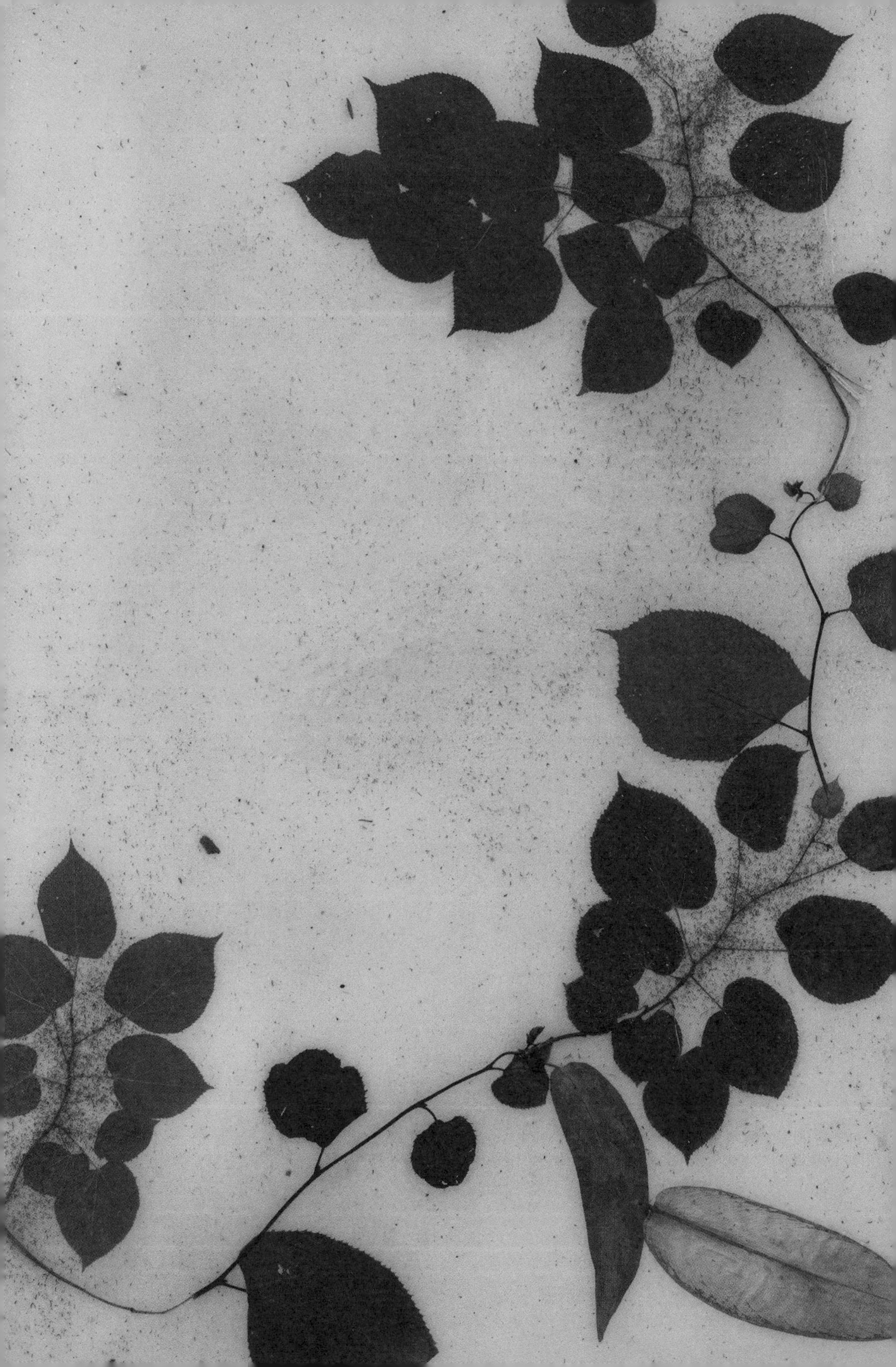

Contents

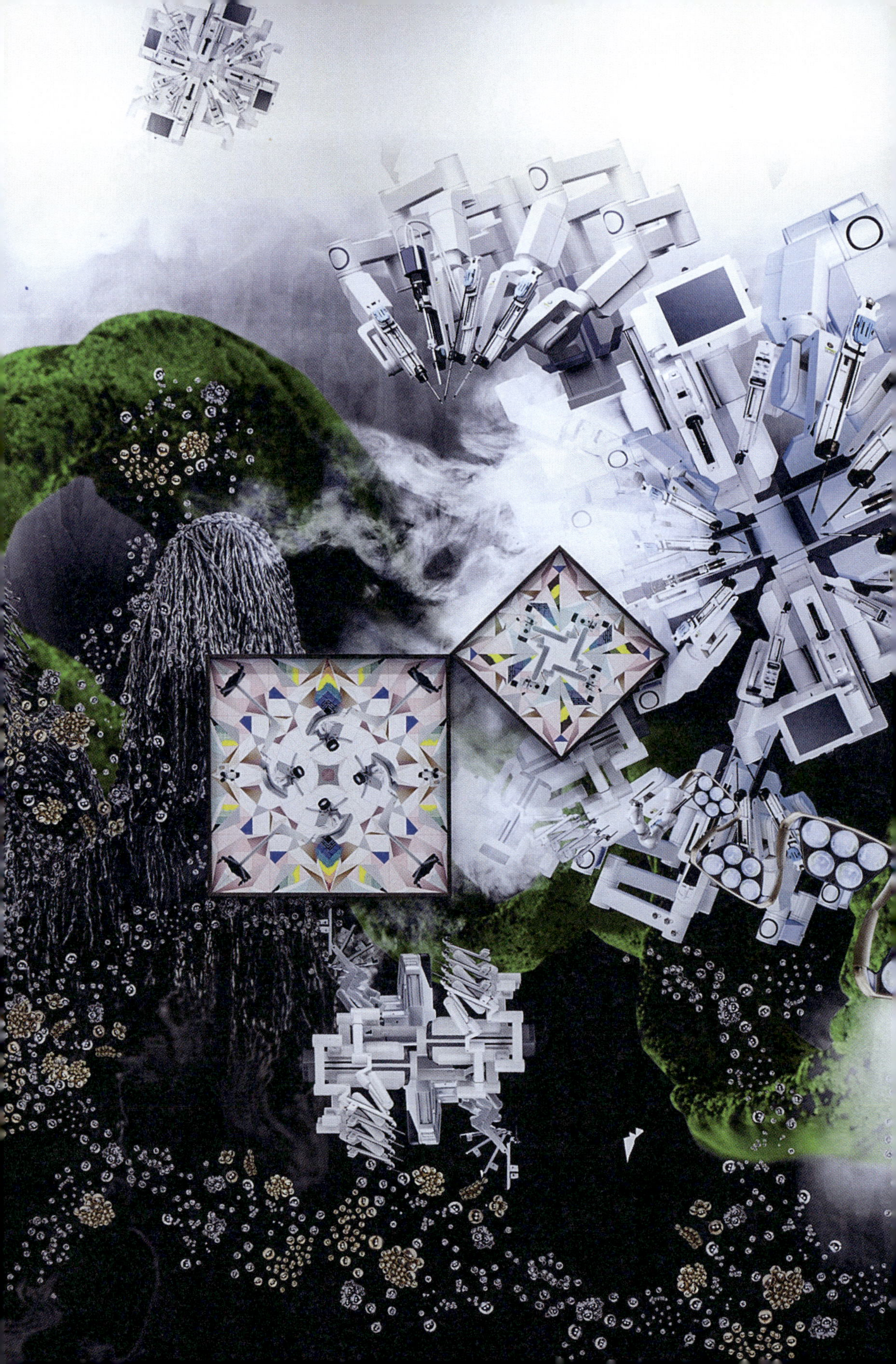

Janine Mileaf
Director's Foreword

In my mental map, "flatness" always has been a hybrid of the contingent and the conscious. It stands as a model counter to the modernist, genre-oriented understanding of dimensionality. Instead, sculptural space may be collapsed to envelop and incubate multiple perspectives. Flatness is an endless fold, cut and paste, or layering.
—HAEGUE YANG

For the first time, *Haegue Yang: Flat Works* gathers together the diversity of the artist's wide-ranging approaches to two-dimensional art in a comprehensive presentation. A survey of several distinct series that range from the early *Hardware Store Collages* of the mid-1990s made from cut-outs of consumer catalogs to the recent *Mesmerizing Mesh* paper collages exploring diverse paper artistry of shamanistic or pagan cultures, *Haegue Yang: Flat Works* provides a broad and deep insight into Yang's ongoing development of ideas around dimensionality that have coexisted with her more recognized sculpture and installation work. A resulting recognition, which connects through early realizations of modernism, is that "flatness" registers a "collapse" of the three-dimensional world as image. This translation causes junctures and elisions of representation that point toward the status of art as fundamentally abstract.

Yang has asserted that she does not make drawings. Instead, her two-dimensional investigations make use of an array of strategies to produce and register marks. For example, she employs cutting, printing both by hand and at commercial scale, indexical projections, chance, creasing, folding, traditional craft, gluing, lacquering, and photography. Through these multiple strategies, Yang questions themes ranging from domesticity and industry to colonialism and climate change. The summary of works included in the exhibition reveal Yang as attentive to sensory experience and grounded in materiality while attuned to specific and timely concerns.

This publication, *Haegue Yang: Flat Works*, provides a substantive and long-overdue analysis of Yang's lesser-known two-dimensional investigations with texts by Orianna Cacchione, Assistant Director and Curator of Exhibitions at the Art, Design & Architecture Museum at University of California, Santa Barbara. Cacchione not only traces the mode of each invention, but she also provides understanding of their intersection with Yang's greater oeuvre, arguing for freedom of thought that is provided by a shift in dimensions. We are grateful to David Khan-Giordano for the sensitive design that clarifies each investigation, and to Edoardo Ghizzoni at Skira for shepherding the project into print. Major support for the publication was provided by Kukje

Gallery, Seoul, with additional help from kurimanzutto, Mexico City and New York, and Galerie Barbara Wien, Berlin. We have benefited greatly from these galleries' significant commitment to the artist.

The capacity to host a retrospective of such an expanse of ideas in a compact format has relied upon the vision of many. For their enormous efforts, we thank the immensely capable studios of Haegue Yang in both Seoul and Berlin, especially Liene Harms for her incomparable management of every detail. The staff of The Arts Club of Chicago, as always, deftly handled the many demands of a complex exhibition. Major funding for the exhibition was provided by Kimberly Querrey and the Smart Family Foundation. For their generous contributions to the Ambition Fund of The Arts Club of Chicago, we are further indebted to Gay-Young Cho, Gary Metzner and Scott Johnson, and Charles Mottier.

Finally, we want to express our deep appreciation for Haegue Yang. Her endless inventiveness, rigorous standards, and uncompromising intellect brought nuance and accomplishment to this project, and we are honored to present this landmark survey of the "flat works."

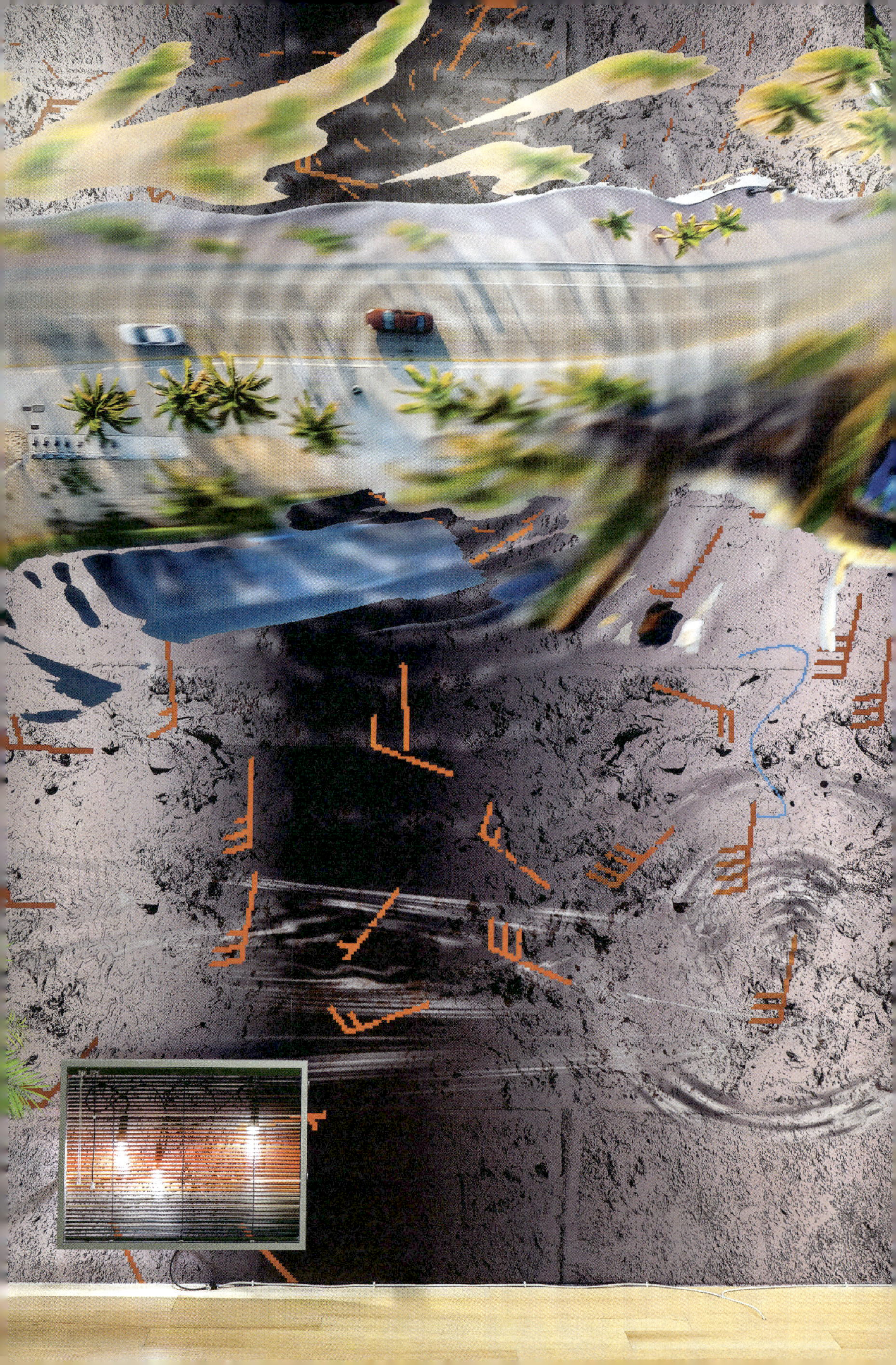

Orianna Cacchione

Non-Parallel Dimensions: Shifting between Haegue Yang's Flat Work and Sculpture

*Exactly: you see you do not even know what Space is.
You think it is of Two Dimensions only; but I have come to
announce to you a Third—height, breadth, and length.*
—EDWIN A. ABBOTT, *FLATLAND*[1]

In conversation, Haegue Yang describes herself as a sculptor, hinting at a medium specificity that is hard to identify in contemporary art let alone in her own work.[2] The prominence and persistence of what she calls "flat works"—artworks most simply described as those in two dimensions—belie the primacy of sculpture in Yang's practice. Since enrolling in art school in Germany in 1994, flat works have remained a constant presence and, in fact, often predate her major sculptural series.

The flat works and sculptures are irrevocably connected; they act in parallel dimensions that allow Yang to experiment with a range of strategies and operations that are often recuperated and exchanged between two and three dimensions. Yet, the flat works contest their own flatness; they open themselves to space—of other dimensions, of objects, of folds and of absence. As such, the flat works are not flat at all, they are sites of compression, paradoxically revealing a depth of space. For Yang, flattening is a "synonym for abstraction"[3] and this abstraction acts across dimensions to infiltrate and deconstruct ways of knowing in contemporary society. Objects, spaces and places alike are flattened and expanded, folded and unfolded, faceted, shifted and made askew. Oscillating between two and three dimensions, Yang challenges standardized systems of organization, production, taxonomy, economy, and movement to unveil the ways in which they limit, order, and structure daily life and suggest other ways of knowing and being in the world.

Arraying Arrangements
Inspired by Yang's frequent trips to the *baumarkt* (hardware store) in her formative years in Frankfurt in the mid-1990s, Yang's earliest flat work series—*Lacquer Paintings* and *Hardware Store Collages*—evince strategies of arrangement that penetrate new modes of production and poor materiality across two and three dimensions. The *Hardware Store Collages* break down the dictionary-like taxonomies that the standardized organization of the hardware stores offered. Cutouts of sinks, bathtubs and toilets [Fig. 1], doorknobs, wires, clocks, mirrors, and trash cans, even fish tanks and fireplaces [Plate 2] are disengaged from the ordered and orderly pages of hardware store catalogues, rearranged

into dynamic lines, groups, circles, and spirals, desperately decontextualized. Started almost simultaneously with the *Hardware Store Collages*, the *Lacquer Paintings* straddle a divide between collage and sculptural process through an exploration of cheap, accessible materials. These "paintings"

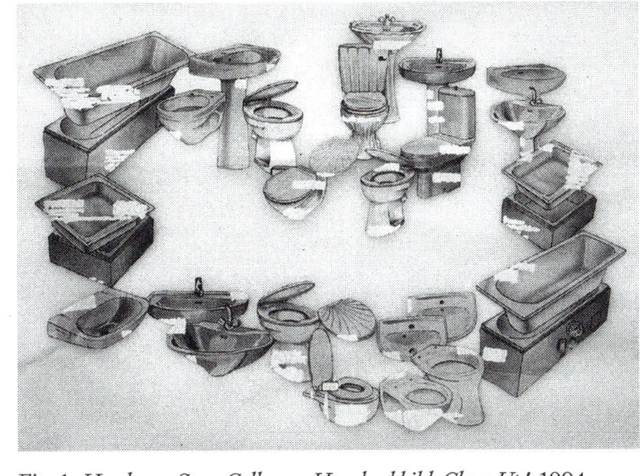

Fig. 1 *Hardware Store Collage – Hornbachbild, Clean Up!*, 1994

operate as an anecdote to more conventional modes of sculpture making—industrial lacquer is poured over the materials left-over in the studio: cut-out grids [Fig. 2], collages of graph paper, and arrangements of discarded objects from seeds to utility knife blades, leaves and flowers and even leftover grocery bags [Plate 17]. Described by Yang as "a very untechnical way of working," lacquer proves an unruly material, saturating each layer until it becomes almost transparent and introducing chance into the process. Often left to dry outside for weeks at a time, the tacky lacquer traps dust and debris while rain and wind impel and shift the surface's texture—preserving and encapsulating not only the materials collaged under its surface, but also traces of the world around it. These serendipitous and spontaneous arrangements document and compress the passing of time and accumulation.

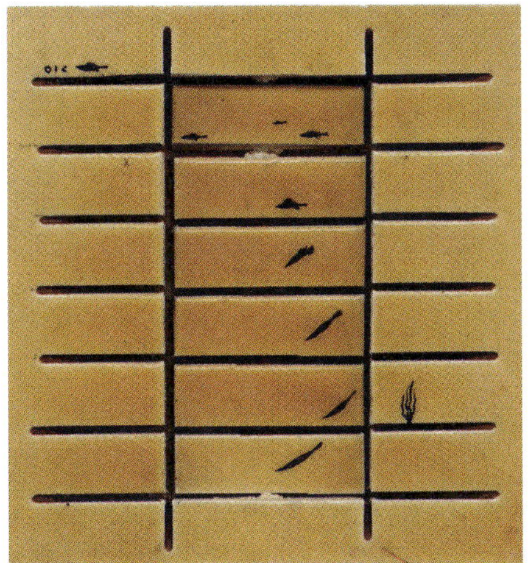

Fig. 2 *The Transformation from Fish to Leaf*, 1994

In these series, the orderly and serialized presentations of mass production and consumption are broken down, complicated by Yang's dizzying arrangements, or perhaps more aptly rearrangements, of very ordinary things. Arrangements appear again and again throughout Yang's practice in two and three dimensions. As Yang describes:

I am often interested in making things by loose association, which can be described by the word "arrangements"; this again

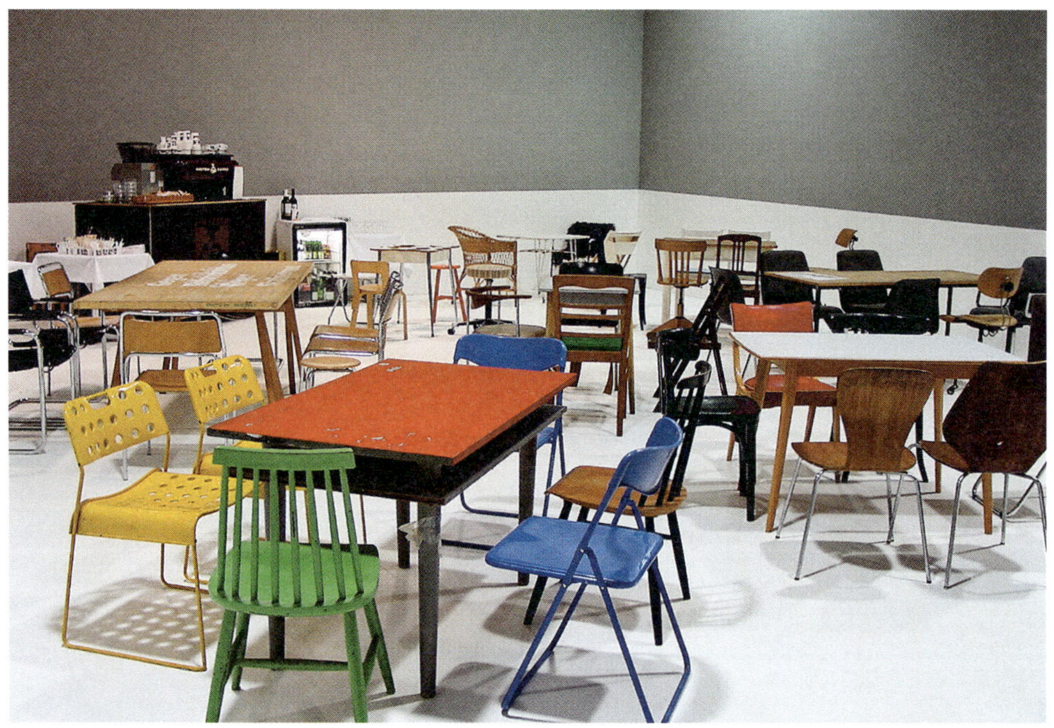

Fig. 3 *VIP's Union*, 2001

allows me to follow a methodology of "take" instead of "make"
. . . I am interested in observing how new compositions arise
while cutting and pasting, which is a non-editing process.
Also "arrangements" applies to the nature of things I take.
Regardless of whether they are events, phenomena, objects,
or images, I am often drawn by the vulnerability of things and
I realize they make me vulnerable as well.[4]

Arrangement operates to catalogue the uncatalogued and
rearrange the ordinarily indexed to upend standard systems of
display, organization, and trade. In the room-scaled installation,
VIP's Union (since 2001) [Fig. 3], Yang tests how to translate this
act of arrangement from the flat surface of collage to three-
dimensional space. First shown at Art Forum Berlin, the
organizers of the now-defunct art fair asked their invited
"very important people" to lend household objects to furnish
the VIP room. Borrowed chairs and tables were matched and
assembled in space to create a kind of landscape—a document
of the "cultural landscape" of Berlin—that transformed the
VIPs from consumers to active participants in the making of

the fair. Furnishing the traditionally luxe lounge with common household items, Yang questions how "very important people" are determined and what they contribute, upending traditional value systems in the art world. This furnishing mirrors the *Hardware Store Collages*, where re-arranging makes vulnerable previously orderly systems of classification, organization, and ultimately valuation. "Vulnerable Arrangements"—where objects are displaced from their typical environment and rearranged in another space—become a persistent occurrence and eventual series in Yang's work. The first, *Series of Vulnerable Arrangements – Version Utrecht* (2006) Fig. 4 creates a sensory encounter or landscape by combining different types of objects in space— venetian blinds, a globe light, two heat lamps, a humidifier, an industrial fan, and two scent dispensers. A perplexing arrangement of objects and sensations makes strange not only the experience of viewing art but also these mundane things, conjuring up questions of how and why they relate to each other. Vulnerable arrangements expose the ways the categorization of objects and experiences are habituated through standard strategies of display and consumption.

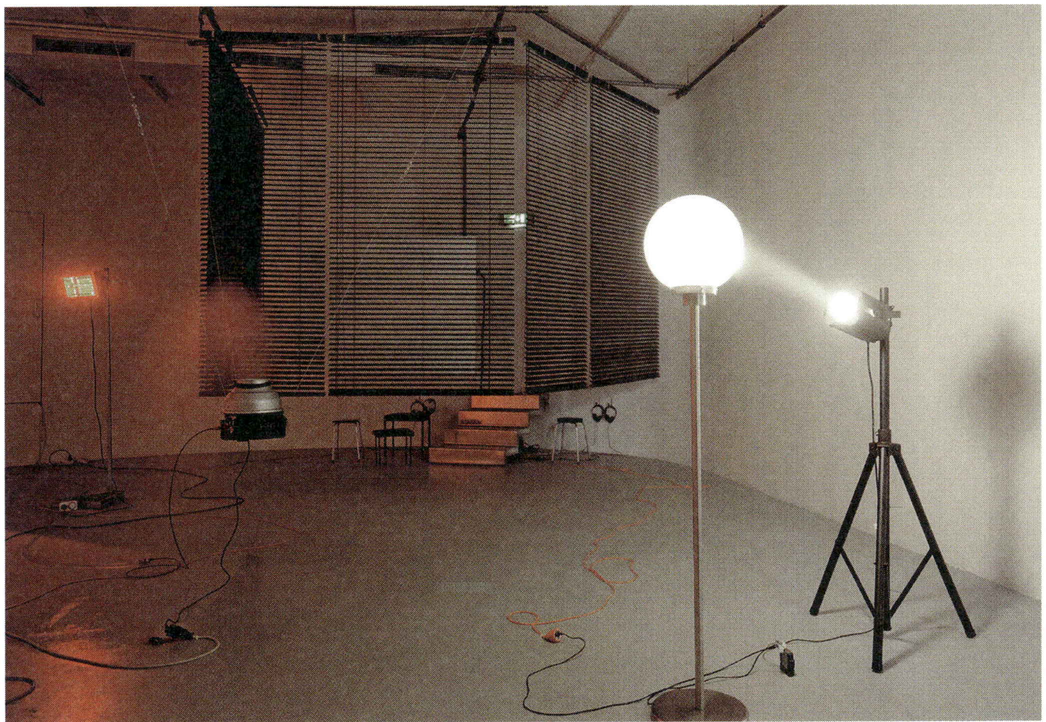

Fig. 4 *Series of Vulnerable Arrangements – Version Utrecht*, 2006

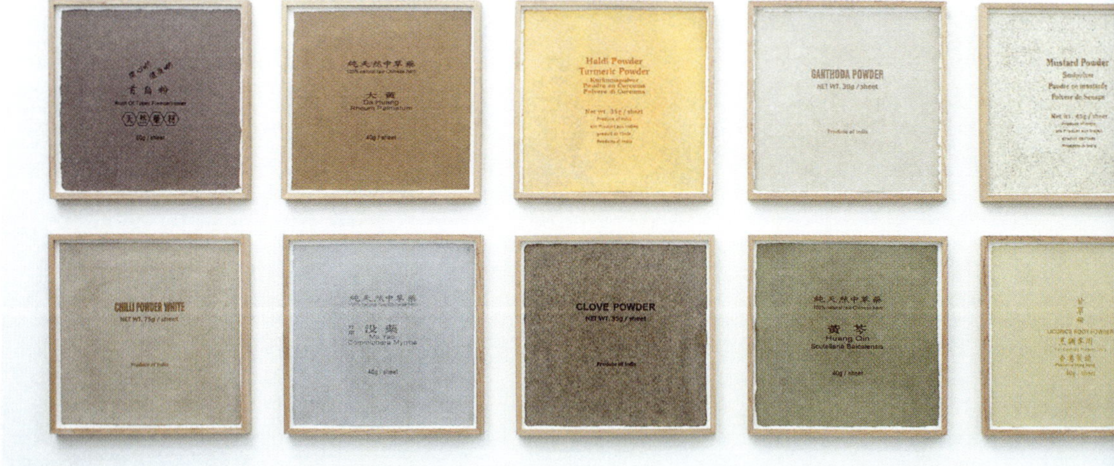
Fig. 5 *Spice Sheets*, 2012

Yang's *Edibles* (since 2012), including *Spice Prints* (since 2012) and *Vegetable Prints* (since 2012), extend this investigation to commodities and how they hold traces of the economic systems that underpin their global circulations. Made during a residency in Singapore's STPI, Yang moves from the hardware store to the spice market, similarly revisiting the ways in which everyday objects are inscribed by and circulate within systems of regulation and power. Spices and vegetables become both the object and materials of these prints. Once more valuable than gold, spices— including cinnamon, ginger, clove, cardamom, turmeric, and chili—are transformed into paper and printed with the labels of their original packaging emphasizing the spices as commodities,

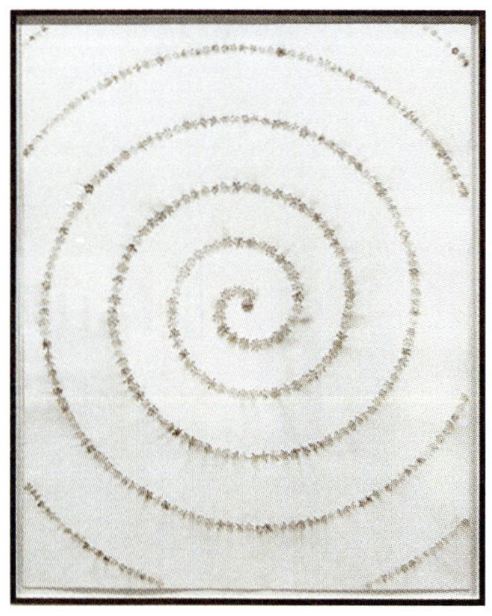
Fig. 6 *Spice Print – Anise Spiral Natural*, 2012

manufactured for global sale ᶠⁱᵍ· ⁵. In other works, star anise flowers and cut vegetables are catalogued into dancing arrangements, twirling, and spiraling on *décalcomanie* prints ᶠⁱᵍ· ⁶. Working with spices grown, processed, and sold around the world, Yang hints at the long history of the spice trade that fueled colonialism and permeates invisible regimes of postcolonial order. In an interview with T. J. Demos, Yang explains, "I can't stop myself from examining the figures and

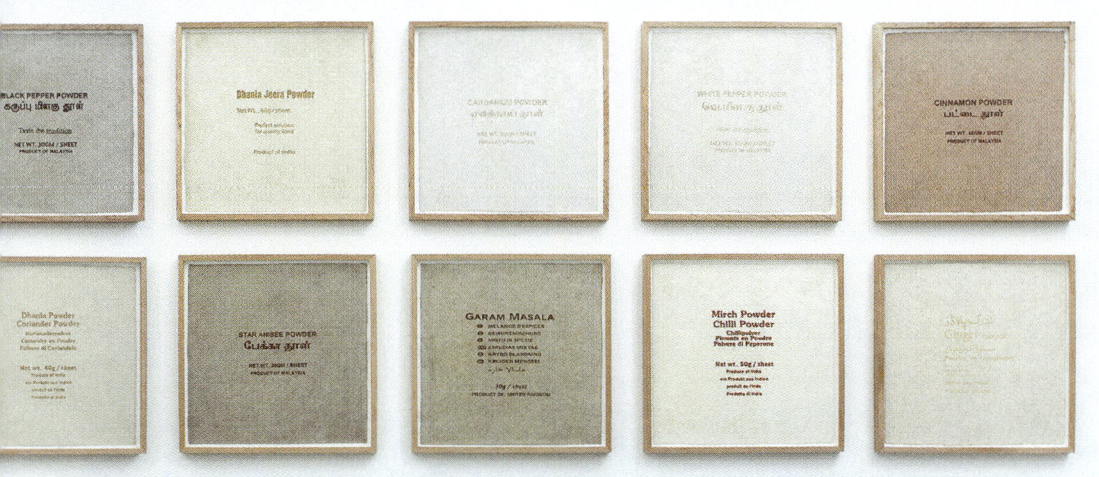

events that seem significant to comprehend the elusive aspects of the colonial circumstances in which we are living today."[5] Colonial circumstances become disguised in economic forms— the spices we use to season our food, the vegetables cultivated around the world, the catalogues we browse, and the repeating and repeatable aisles at grocery, hardware, and furniture stores that display stacks of merchandise ready for easy consumption. Yang's playful and often ecstatic arrangements reveal the hidden histories of standardized forms of display, exchange, and postcolonial order.

Folding Follies

In Yang's flat and video works, *Cove* (2004) and *Video Trilogy* (2004–2006), origami stealthily emerges as a dimension shifter. Folding and unfolding paper allows Yang to move between two- and three-dimensional space as flat planes of paper are creased and assembled into polyhedrons and then unfolded into flat sheets again. Her use of origami is first documented in *Video Trilogy*, a series of video essays filmed during Yang's travels in Seoul, Europe, and Brazil that reflect on movement, travel, immigration, transience, and place. In each, images of different cities—walking along unlabeled streets, vignettes of urban objects, rare interior scenes—are combined with the voiceover of an unseen narrator who recounts contemplations and observations of places, relationships, and community. Yet there is a disparity

11

between the voiceover and the images moving on the screen. In the first video in the series, *Unfolding Places* (2004) ^{Fig. 7}, origami forms float in puddles on the street, they blow in the wind as the narrator divulges a story from a bus ride in London. At the end of the film, the same origami objects travel to a studio, placed on a white ground while an invisible hand begins to spray black paint on them, and a voice narrates "In the midst of passing scenery, a series of unnamed spaces emerge as new places. Going through places. Reaching a place. Leaving the place and hitting the road." The origami shapes are out of place, just as the voiceover seems out of sync with the passing frames and by extension the viewer.

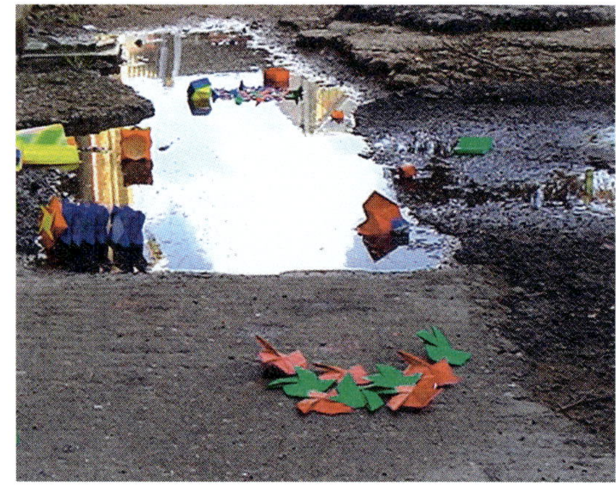

Fig. 7 *Unfolding Places*, 2004 (video still)

How do we reconcile these registers of voice, moving image, and origami? Origami acts as an allegory of moving in space. These videos project the experience of moving between different places in a globalized society, hinting at the familiar and yet obscuring it, suggesting proximity while emphasizing isolation. Spaces converge with travel stories, narratives and places are folded back upon themselves, unfolded and then folded again. Here folding and unfolding act not just as a means of flattening and reconstructing space, but as a way of connecting places and structuring the relationships between them as if a geometry, a mesmerizing matrix. This relationality of origami becomes an operative strategy of making sense out of place and time. This shifting of dimensions—the convergence between flat planes, objects in space, actual locations, their shadows, traces, and obstinate absence—becomes an entirely innovative means to document and project how we move through the world. As if the multifaceted planes of the origami objects become new angles and intersecting modes of vision, of being in and out of space and time.

Cove ^{Fig. 8} repurposes the large and long white paper sheet on which the origami arrangement in *Unfolding Places* was laid and spray-painted black into a hanging scroll-like painting.

12

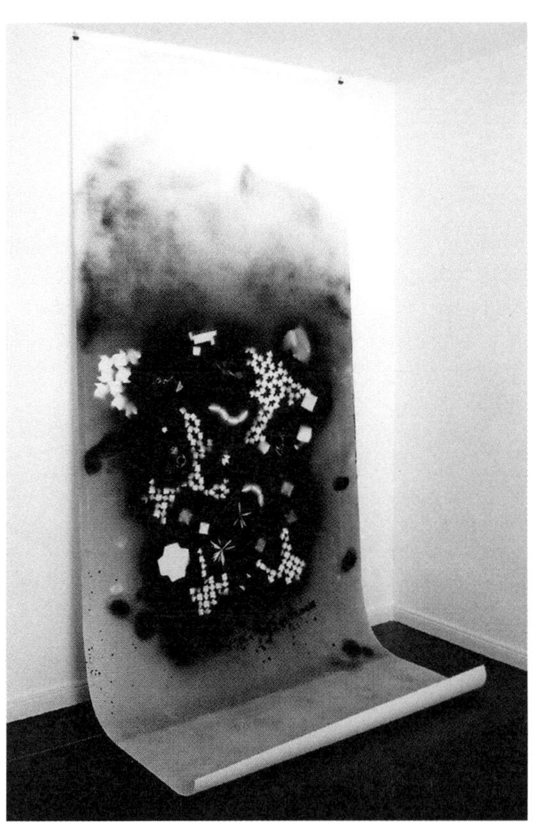

Capturing only the contours of absent origami objects, the work is a confounding document of abstracted traces and shadows that withhold the possibility of fully revealing their referents. This is codified, as it were, in a series started in 2007, *Non-Foldings* ^{Plates 23–26}, which similarly record the negative spaces around an arrangement of origami shapes in varying opacities of black spray paint. Doryun Chong has argued this other dimension in Yang's work—non-folding— "manifests itself visually and physically as shadows or shades, which operate as autonomous, self-sufficient beings, banishing the original, positive shapes in the realm of the undetectable, as if the original never existed in the first place."[6] The folded shape vanishes, its contours hinted at through the different intensities of black. In *Restrained Courage* (2004), the second video in *Video Trilogy*, the narrator declares: "'Vanishing' can be understood in different ways. The vanishing I speak of is both a literal vanishing and a kind of isolation. This state implies an extreme break in the course of life or time." If folding allows new proximities to emerge, non-folding provides an escape, an extreme flattening of space and time that leads to its own disappearance.

Made in 2006, *Gymnastics of the Foldables* ^{Plate 54} suggests the possibility of other objects folding in space. Captured in 15 photographs, the humble, banal laundry rack becomes personified as a performer—its flat wire appendages transformed into arms and legs. Its ability to fold and hold varying poses define its functionality and yet these graceful gestures are overlooked in daily life. Yang assertively proclaims the sculptural-ness of the made-to-store-flat laundry rack in the series,

Non-Indépliables (Non-Unfoldables) ^{Fig. 9}. Yang compares these
to Alexander Rodchenko's *Spatial Constructions* (1919–1921),
collapsible sculptures made by cutting thin sheets of wood
into concentric shapes and then fanning them out into three
dimensions. The *Non-Indépliables*, however, resist their return to
two dimensions; the racks are adorned in tight garments made
from solid-colored cloth that freezes the gymnastic shape in
space. Cloaked, the humble object and its daily functionality
vanish from sight and are instead replaced by the resulting
colorful abstract sculpture created with intersecting planes in
space. Laundry racks and display racks form a persistent support
for Yang to build kinetic sculptures that repeat again and again
from the *Non-Indépliables*. These sculptures abstract the labor of
housework—folding clothes, folding laundry racks compressed to
folding paper—shifting its gaze from the outward focus on travel
and movement to the interiority of domestic spaces and daily life.

Yang transforms this operation of folding into installations
created with venetian blinds, developing new immersive
environments that both contain and project the viewer into the
structures, folds, and angles of origami. Venetian blinds are first

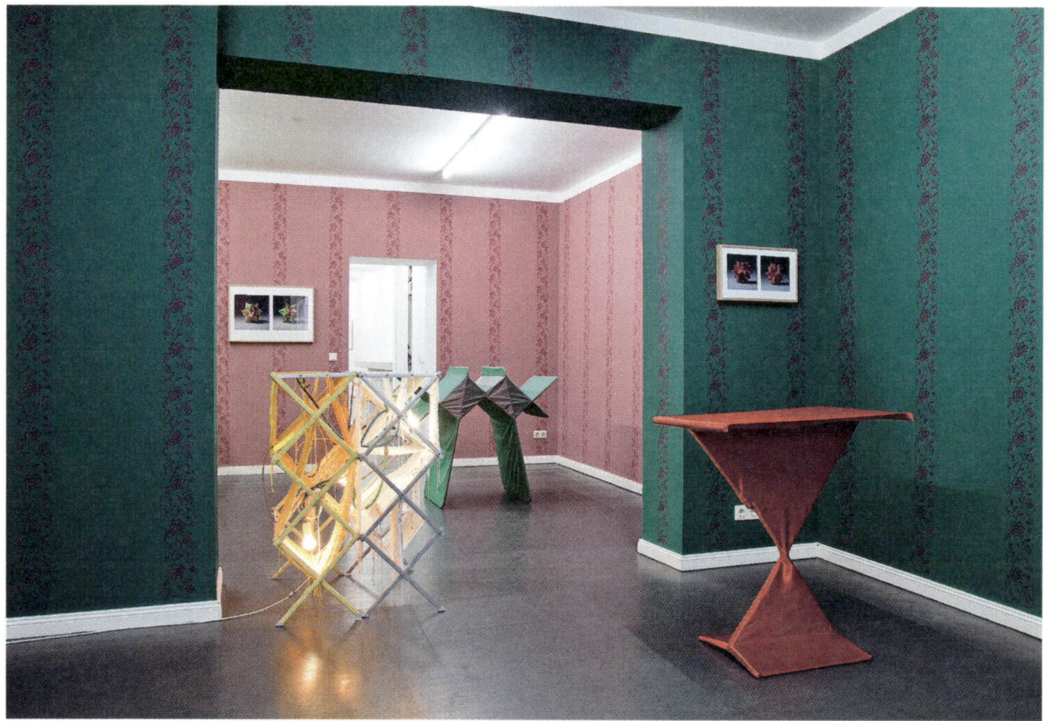

Fig. 9 *Non-Indépliables*, 2009–2010

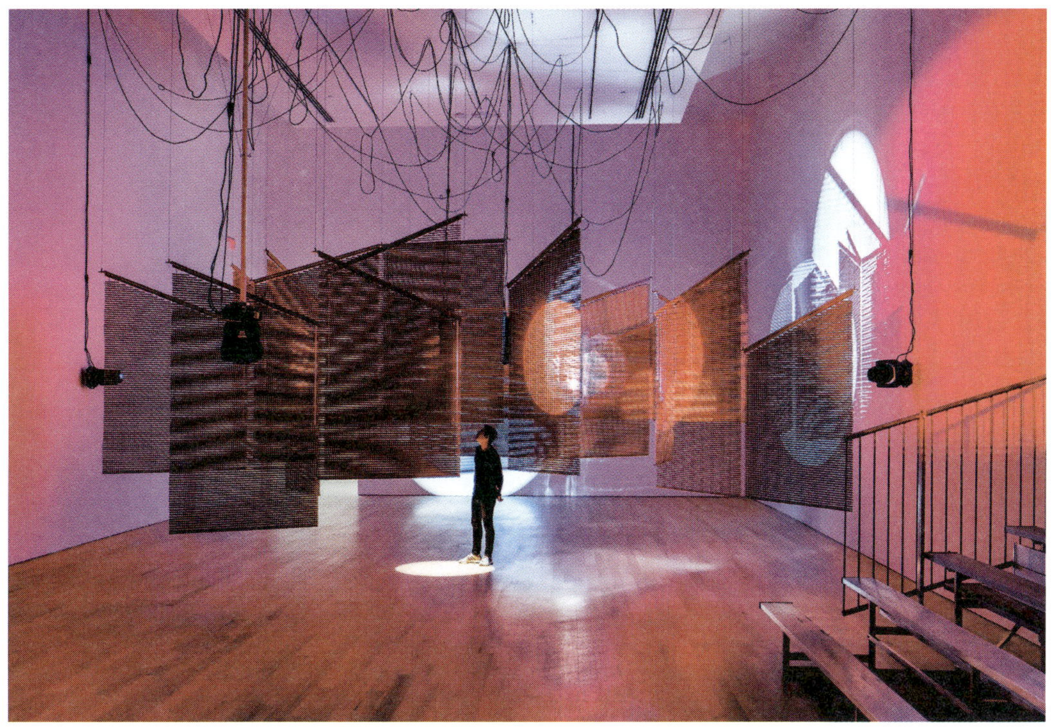

Fig. 10 *Red Broken Mountainous Labyrinth*, 2008

employed in *Series of Vulnerable Arrangements – Version Utrecht* (2006) as screens that seem to frame or cordon off a space inside a room. From this installation, Yang begins to employ more and more venetian blinds, dangling them down from the ceiling, pairing and parting and angling them together in complex geometric configurations. Origami is repeatedly connected to these installations: Nicolas Bourriaud describes them as being arranged "according to a law of *folds*;"[7] Doryun Chong attests that "sculpting is not done by carving or molding, it may be accomplished by folding and unfolding;"[8] and Yasmil Raymond suggests that the layout of the blinds takes their shape from "the creases left on a piece of paper previously used for origami."[9] In works like, *Red Broken Mountainous Labyrinth* (2008) [Fig. 10], flat venetian blinds are removed from their function as window coverings and choreographed in space to create landscapes. The faceting planes in bright red conceal, connect, and construct spaces, entangling the viewer in a maze. Standing within the installation that is both immersive and architectural, thrust into the red of blinds and the red of a tracing light, your view and relation to the surrounding room are obscured. A landscape merges from these flat objects floating in space, creating a subtle shift in dimension. Yang's installation works on the viewer through these folds, where suddenly through a crease or the faceting together of two planes, your point of view becomes skewed—altering your position in space, art history, dimensionality.

Enveloping Abstractions

In many ways a negation of origami, the *Trustworthies* series began in 2010 through the act of unfolding—opening security envelopes to reveal the miniature patterns of faint crosshatching, insignia, logos, bank names, and even recycle signs that repeat endlessly to hide confidential information within. These papers form the substrate for collages, ripped bands placed on top of each other in cascading geometric shapes. The repeated and repeating parallel lines of the *Trustworthies* mirror the individual slats strung together in the venetian blind works. Often the strips shift and angle to create intersecting planes—flattened renditions of the venetian blind installations. They are perhaps the flattest of the flat works, the most overtly abstract and ornamental, yet they provide a sense of depth through the optical illusion of layering. Yang's titles for the *Trustworthies* often suggest contemporary koans—including *Scanning Hot Inner Values* (2019) [Plate 30], *Prosthetic Locomotion* (2018) and *Drone Swarm in Knots* (2018)—establishing a tension, contradiction even, with the seemingly abstract collages. These riddles suggest speculative fiction—hidden narratives under the overlapping grids and gradients that might be solved if only seen from the right angle.

This folding, flattening, and abstracting of narratives run through Yang's earlier video works, like *Video Trilogy*, but begins to take on new forms in the *Trustworthies* and *Rotating Notes* (2010), another series started in 2010. As Yang describes, "for me, abstraction is not antinarrative, it is not a language that attempts to negate narration but rather allows a narrative to be achieved without constituting its own limits."[10] Yang mashes up images and narratives alike—shifting how they are catalogued, taking and remaking, rearranging them—precisely through their compression. In the kinetic relief sculptures, *Rotating Notes* [Fig. 11], magnetic boards are pinned with snippets of photocopied research related to postcolonial entanglements, diasporic authors, political movements, and ancient art histories. When spun, the disparate documents and discrete images blur into a single abstracted form, meshed together beyond comprehension, obscuring the rational presentation of information. The sculptural objects are adorned with information as if decorated, shifting the register of research to ornamentation, and then

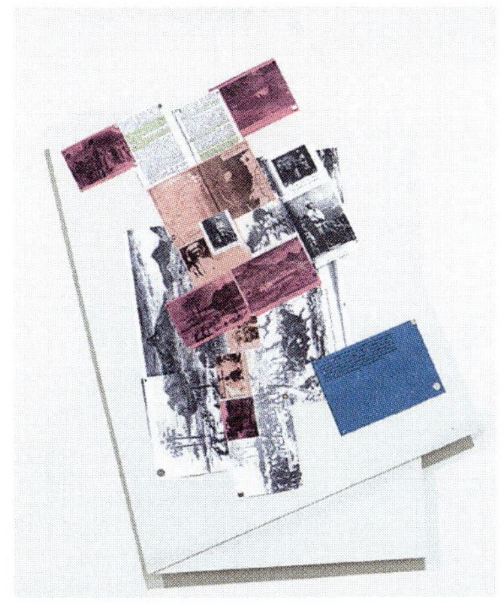

Fig. 11 *Rotating Notes* (detail), 2010

to oblivion as the plate spins faster and faster. Both an act of "unlearning" and free association, Yang opens up the hierarchies of knowledge typically codified through scientific and historical narratives to allow the viewer to make their own reading or reject it entirely, asking them to take and make as she has done.

When the *Trustworthies* are hung on the wall, they twist, turn, and tilt in space with each other; they double, triple, and quadruple as if modules to spread and stretch along flat walls, expanding beyond their frames with decals and painted sections that link and loop as if elaborate diagrams. The individual *Trustworthies* included in *Central Composition in Explosion – Trustworthy #184* (2012–2013) [Fig. 12] exceed their frames and seamlessly, almost surreptitiously engross an entire wall.

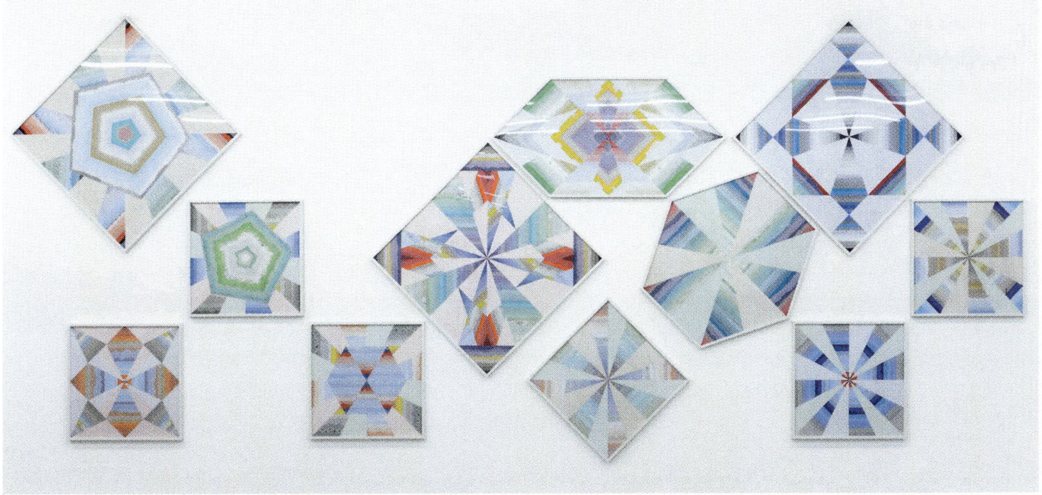

Fig. 12 *Central Composition in Explosion – Trustworthy #184*, 2012–2013

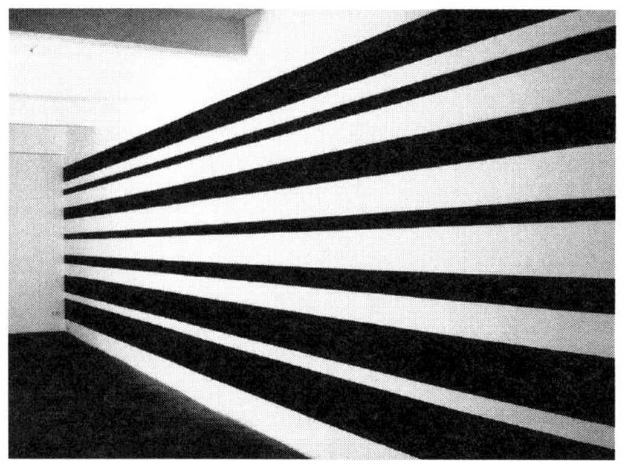
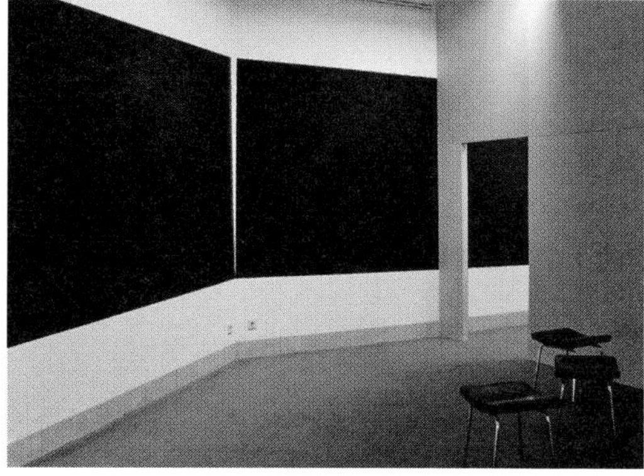

Fig. 13 *Munich Tilt*, 2000

Fig. 14 *Shifted Tilt*, 2001

As described in the catalogue for *Family of Equivocations*, these presentations of multiple *Trustworthies* seem "environmental, however flat the collaged surface may seem. It is perhaps the most visually driven room as it aspires to 'design' the walls."[11] These designed walls that writhe with movement relate back to earlier wall paintings. In *Munich Tilt* (2000) [Fig. 13] and *Shifted Tilt* (2001) [Fig. 14], black stripes and blocks are tilted slightly, in fact exactly to one degree, as if anticipating the angled planes and kissing corners of the *Trustworthies*. These bands and blocks askew the hard parallels and right angles of the wall and shift the determinacy of the viewer in space.

Seen this way, it is not a surprise that Yang begins to work with wallpaper that envelopes and immerses spaces, remaking the decorative material with abstracted narratives. In fact, the earliest wallpaper, *Field of Teleportation* [Fig. 15], reproduced the *Trustworthies* floating among photographs of Yang's other artworks and installed around sculptures in the same gallery, almost confoundingly flattening the flat works even further. These reproductions compress curatorial strategies to create new diagrams and schematics of relationality between artworks and backdrops for actual artworks in space. This shuttling between the real and the reproduced opens new narrative structures of indeterminacy created precisely through this extreme compression of space into exceedingly flat, complex photo collages. *Incantations – Entwinement, Endurance, and Extinction* (2022) [Plate 31], like almost all of the wallpapers, obliquely addresses climate change through the collapsing of references and referents, past artworks, and images precisely through this act of flattening.

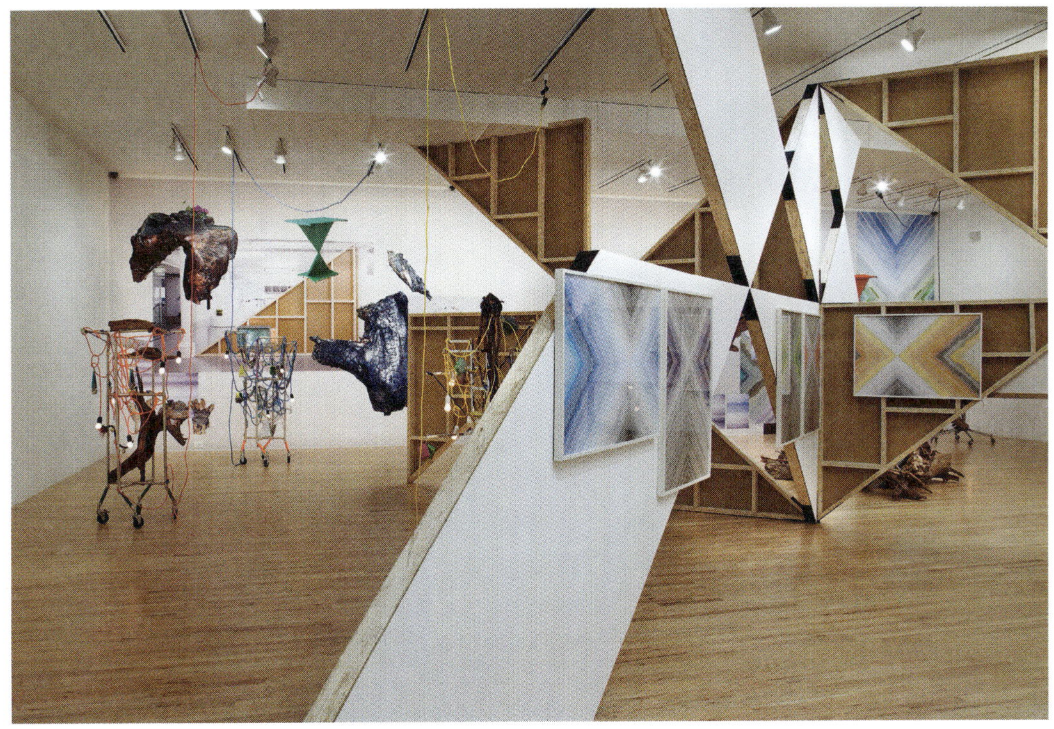

Fig. 15 *Field of Teleportation*, 2011

Scientific treatises collide with shamanistic knowledge and intuition to create strange, abstracted landscapes ripe with free association that beckon the viewer to start to parse together and make sense of the visual overload presented. The conflation of abstraction, ornamentation, and decoration in the immersive wallpapers can no longer be understood as landscapes. Instead the massive scale and proliferation of information and images suggest environments, atmospheres, climates—not discrete locations that can be folded back on themselves, but rather complex interconnected systems disguised as ornamental through their appropriation of design and décor and sheer visual overload.

Mystic Mediations

Another system for knowing and making sense of the world, shamanism infiltrates Yang's working methods conceptually and through craft practices in both sculptural and flat work series. The first to overtly reference this seeking of other forms of knowledge, *Seoul Guts – Medicine Man* (2010) ^{Fig. 16} anthropomorphizes another genre of *Vulnerable Arrangements*, in which clothing racks are decorated with the mass-produced detritus of contemporary

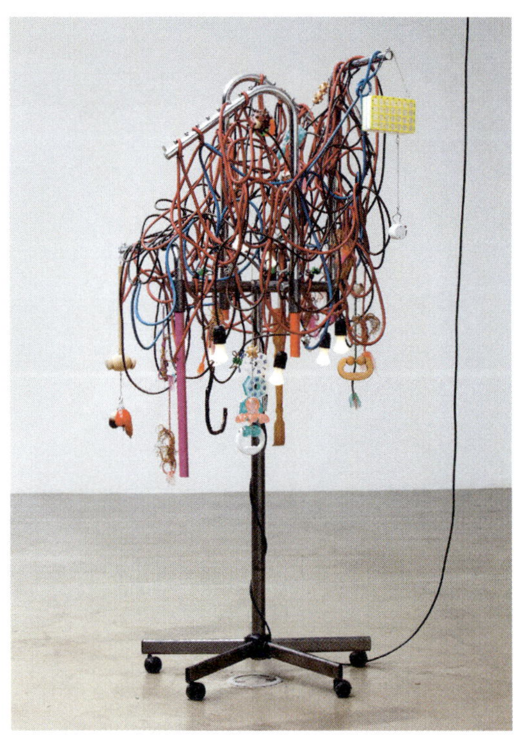
Fig. 16 *Seoul Guts – Medicine Man*, 2010

life—lights, cables, yarn, zip ties, rope, tinsel, plastic funnels, shells, origami shapes, and hot pads. Festooned with bells, dried ginseng, and garlic, pill boxes and red and blue cords and cables, *Seoul Guts – Medicine Man* points to Yang's emerging interest in shamanistic traditions through both its title and the selection of objects frequently activated in shamanistic rituals, while still describing the contemporary urban hypochondriac life of Seoul. From a single "Medicine Man" to an entire series of *Medicine Men* (2010) paired with *Female Natives* (2010) Fig. 17, Yang begins to recuperate folk and spiritual traditions as alternative knowledge systems that can upend canonic hierarchies through

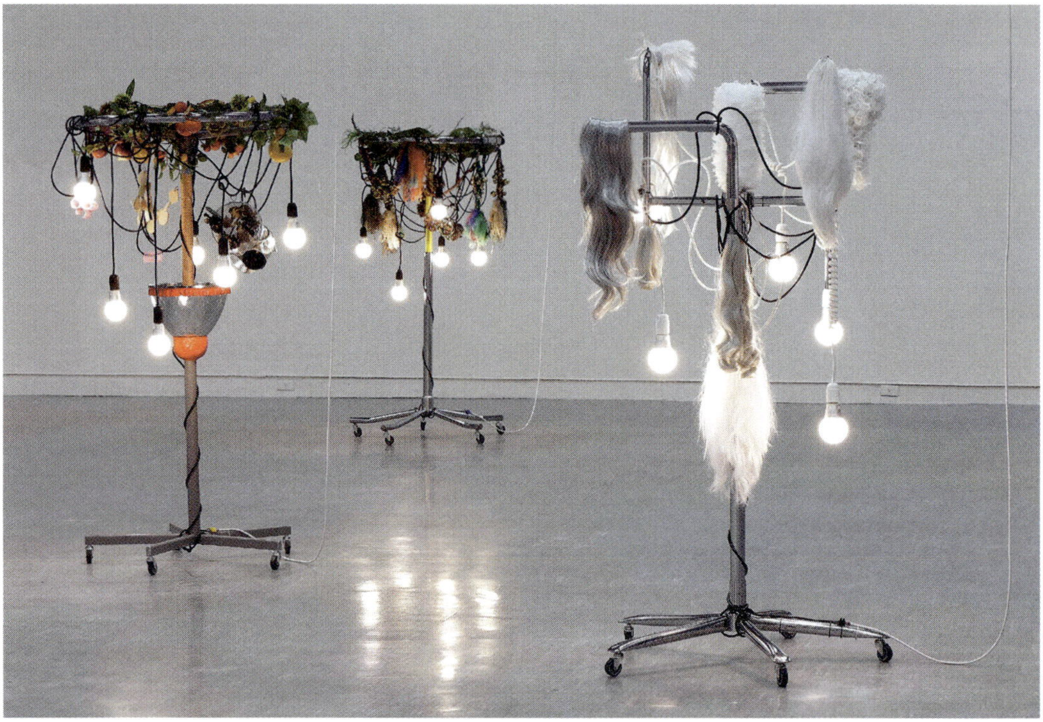

Fig. 17 *Female Natives*, 2010 and *Medicine Men*, 2010 (detail)

the transformation and inclusion of ceremonial objects and indigenous Korean crafts into her sculptures. She incorporates bells—often used to convene ritual ceremonies—to cover entire shapes and structures creating sonic objects. Intended to be worn, touched, and moved to activate their sonic ring, they elicit sensorial experiences.

In *The Intermediates* series ^{Fig. 18} from 2015, she and her team learned from a Korean artisan and produced sculptures on casters formed from the tying and weaving of plastic artificial straw to create shapes both tightly composed and shaggily piled. Inspired by the Japanese and Korean custom of wrapping trees with straw in winter, the sculptures combine "primitive farming materials . . . and ancient hand-weaving techniques" to address the coexistence of man and nature.[12]

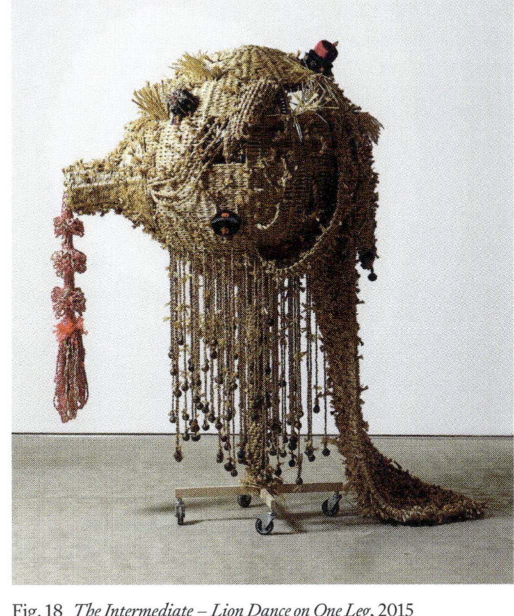

Fig. 18 *The Intermediate – Lion Dance on One Leg*, 2015

Most recently, Yang has turned this interest to two dimensions, employing the folk traditions of paper cutting to create kaleidoscopic collages of transparent *hanji* paper that are often adorned with leaves, reed sticks, and sometimes even graph paper. In *Brier Teardrop Formation – Mesmerizing Mesh #39* (2021) ^{Fig. 19} five dancing figures materialize from the center point in folds and cuts of white paper, reaching toward different points and intricate shapes cut into pink *hanji* and graph paper. The *Mesmerizing Mesh* series (since 2021) reassembles iconic focal references from Japanese Shinto and Korean shamanistic paper cutting and folding practices—a subtle nod to the strategy of arrangement first observed in the *Hardware Store Collages* and *Lacquer Paintings*.

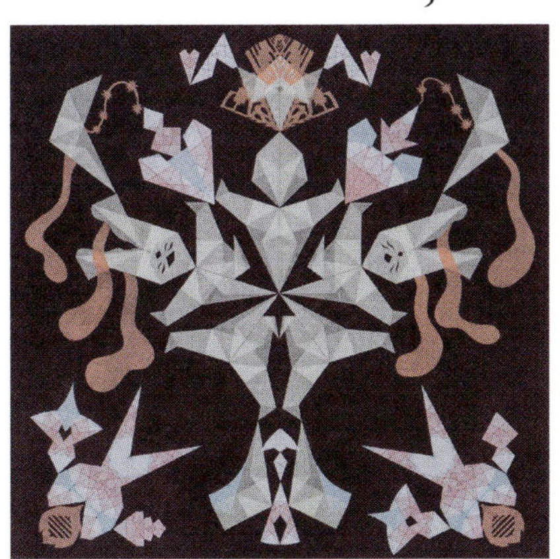

Fig. 19 *Brier Teardrop Formation – Mesmerizing Mesh #39*, 2021

Here, Yang summons shamanistic beliefs that connect and
mediate between spirits, deities, and humans in order to "blow a
soul or spirit" into the poor material of the paper.[13] Puncturing
holes into the *hanji* allows it to breathe[14] and opens the collages
to a shifting between dimensions, life, and death, presence
and absence, and cosmic spaces that evades standard means of
knowing. Connecting Korean and Japanese paper cutting to
seemingly relevant practices in China, Mexico, India, Ukraine, Poland, and Belarus, Yang grasps onto the almost universal use of papercutting in rituals, celebrations, and ceremonies. *Spiritual-Powered Soul Stick – Mesmerizing Mesh #28* (2021) [Fig. 20] embodies the ways in which practices connect and mediate between dimensions. Depicting the fringed "head" and streaming "skirt" of a shaman's Shinjang Stick used to summon the Deity of Longevity, Yang evokes the importance of ritual for creating community and of "making oneself at home in the world."[15]

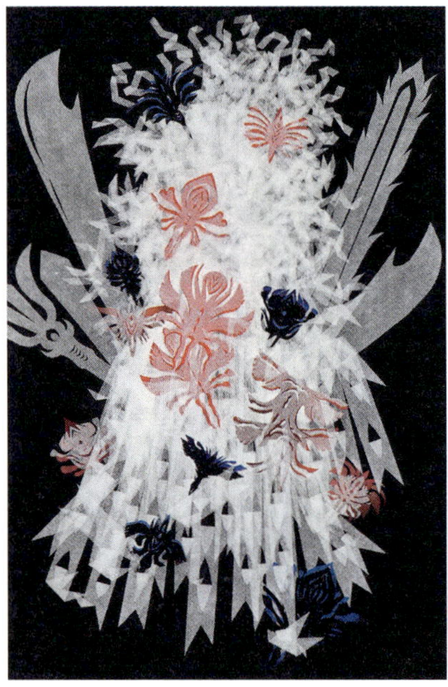

Fig. 20 *Spiritual-Powered Soul Stick – Mesmerizing Mesh #28*, 2021

Harnessing what Yang calls a "mystic leap," *Mesmerizing Mesh*
projects other ways of knowing and being in the world beyond
rational, scientific, perhaps even modern means. Instead,
they conjure and arouse ancient models of collective, non-
institutionalized belief systems and adaptation, like Korean
shamanism that freely takes and incorporates practices and
principles from Buddhism, Confucianism, Taoism, animism,
feng shui, and fortune-telling.[16] At stake are the ways in which
Yang recuperates these othered systems of knowledge—often
indigenous practices that were suppressed by colonial regimes—
to reassess modernism. Yang frequently evokes Sol LeWitt's
statement in "Sentences on Conceptual Art," "Conceptual Artists
are mystics rather than rationalists. They leap to conclusions that
logic cannot reach."[17] These material and discursive intersections
of indigenous knowledge, craft practices, shamanistic traditions,

and Western modernism begin to displace colonial hierarchies and bodies of knowledge. They wedge themselves between dimensions—flat planes of cut paper and woven spheres of artificial raffia—crossing borders between artifice, ornamentation, and authenticity.

Shifting between dimensions in flat works, sculptures, videos, and installations, abstraction emerges as a reconfiguration of diverse referents, reordered in ways that remove contexts and narratives to create new sites of free expression and association. From arrangements to mystic leaps, Yang interjects our experience of globalization and capitalistic production with a buoyant abstraction that opens to ecology, nature, and shamanism and shifts from a post-colonial to planetary order. Perhaps one can think of this as a shift from folding places as landscapes to climates and atmospheres, positing the possibility of other dimensions that Yang might begin to explore. Evoking the late 19th-century science fiction novel, *Flatland*, that famously imagined the existence of separate societies in two and three dimensions, this might be put another way. Experiencing the third dimension for the first time, the Line exclaims to the Sphere: "Then, yielding to our intellectual onset, the gates of the Sixth dimension, shall fly open; after that a Seventh, and then an Eighth."[18]

Notes

1 Edwin A. Abbott, *Flatland* (London, New York, Victoria, Toronto, Auckland: Penguin Books, 1987), 66.
2 Conversation with the Author on September 11, 2023.
3 Ibid.
4 Haegue Yang as quoted in Eugie Joo, "A Conversation" in *Haegue Yang: Anthology 2006–2018, Tightrope Walking and Its Wordless Shadow*, ed. Bruna Roccasalva (Milan: Skira, 2019), 145–146.
5 Haegue Yang as quoted in T.J. Demos, "Accommodating the Epic Dispersion" in *Accommodating the Epic Dispersion – On Non-cathartic Volume of Dispersion*, ed. Julienne Lorz, part of the series *DER ÖFFENTLICHKEIT – Von den Freunden Haus der Kunst* (Munich: Haus der Kunst; Cologne: Verlag der Bachhandlung Walther König, 2013), 71.
6 Doryun Chong , "A Small Dictionary for Haegue Yang" in *Haegue Yang: Anthology 2006–2018, Tightrope Walking and Its Wordless Shadow*, ed. Bruna Roccasalva (Milan: Skira, 2019), 89.
7 Nicolas Bourriaud, "Unfolding Experiences: Haegue Yang and Sculpture Today" in *Haegue Yang: Shooting the Elephant 象 Thinking the Elephant*, Hyunsun Tae, ed. (Seoul: Leeum Museum of Art, 2015), 30.
8 Doryun Chong, "Movement Studies" in *Haegue Yang: Anthology 2006–2018, Tightrope Walking and Its Wordless Shadow*, ed. Bruna Roccasalva (Milan: Skira, 2019), 170.
9 Yasmil Raymond, "Haegue Yang" in *Domus*, no. 922, February 2009, 125.
10 Haegue Yang as interviewed in Clara Kim, "Vulnerability for an Exploration" in *Art in Asia* (May–June 2009), 45.
11 *Haegue Yang: Family of Equivocations* (Strasbourg: L'Aubette 1928 and the Musée d'Art Moderne et Contemporain de Strasbourg, 2013), 121.
12 Hyunsun Tae, "Haegue Yang: Landscapes beyond Venetian Blinds" in *Haegue Yang: Shooting the Elephant 象 Thinking the Elephant*, Hyunsun Tae, ed. (Seoul: Leeum Museum of Art, 2015), 10.
13 Haegue Yang, *Mesmerizing Mesh* (Seoul: Kukje Gallery, 2021), 7.
14 Haegue Yang, *Mesmerizing Mesh – Paper Leap* (Berlin: Wiens Verlag, 2022), 7.
15 Byung-Chul Han, *The Disappearance of Rituals: A Topology of the Present*, trans. by Daniel Steur (Cambridge, UK: Polity Press, 2020), 2.
16 Haegue Yang, *Mesmerizing Mesh – Paper Leap* (Berlin: Wiens Verlag, 2022), 13.
17 Sol LeWitt, "Sentences on Conceptual Art," in Alexander Alberro and Blake Stimson, ed., *Conceptual Art: A Critical Anthology* (Cambridge, MA/London: The MIT Press, 1999), 106.
18 Edwin A. Abbott, *Flatland* (London, New York, Victoria, Toronto, Auckland: Penguin Books, 1987), 83.

Figures

1 *Hardware Store Collage – Hornbachbild, Clean Up!*, 1994. Clippings from hardware store catalogues on tracing paper, whiteout. Dimensions unknown.
2 *The Transformation from Fish to Leaf*, 1994. Chipboard, wood varnish, paint. 20 × 21 × 3.5 cm. Collection Meike Behm and Peter Lütje, Lingen (Ems).
3 *VIP's Union*, 2001. Chairs and tables. Dimensions variable. Installation view of design commissioned for the VIP Lounge at the 6th Art Forum Berlin, Berlin, Germany, 2001.
4 *Series of Vulnerable Arrangements – Version Utrecht*, 2006. Aluminum venetian blinds, various sensory devices, cable. Dimensions variable. Installation view of *Unevenly*, BAK – basis voor actuele kunst, Utrecht, Netherlands, 2006. Collection of M+, Hong Kong. Photo: Ernst Moritz.
5 *Spice Sheets*, 2012. Spice screen print, STPI handmade spices paper, 20 various spices and herbs, framed. 20 parts, 44 × 44 cm each. Ingredients: ginger powder, chili powder, dhania powder, garam masala, ganthoda powder, dhania jeera powder, mustard powder, cardamom powder, white chili powder, clove powder, black pepper powder, white pepper powder, turmeric powder, star anise powder, cinnamon powder, huang qin, root of tuber fleeceflower, da huang, licorice root powder, mo yao. Produced at STPI – Creative Workshop & Gallery, Singapore. Courtesy of Singapore Tyler Print Institute. Photo: Chua Cher Him, Singapore.
6 *Spice Print – Anise Spiral Natural*, 2012. Embossing, natural dye, STPI handmade paper, star anise, framed. 174.5 × 139 cm. Produced at

STPI – Creative Workshop & Gallery, Singapore. Private collection, Seoul. Photo: Chua Cher Him, Singapore.

7 *Unfolding Places*, 2004 (video stills). Single channel DV-PAL, color, sound. 18'15" minutes. Filmed in London and Seoul. Voiceover: Helen Cho (English); Christina Stockhofe (German). Part of *Video Trilogy*, 2004–2006.

8 *Cove*, 2004. Spray paint on paper. 359 × 150 cm. Installation view of *Unfolding Places*, Galerie Barbara Wien, Berlin, Germany, 2004. Private collection, Baltimore. Photo: Roman März.

9 *Non-Indépliables*, 2009–2010. Drying rack, fabric, knitting yarn, light bulbs, cable, zip ties, terminal strips. Dimensions variable. Installation view of *Closures*, Galerie Barbara Wien, Berlin, Germany, 2010. Design of the walls by Jimmie Durham. Photo: Nick Ash.

10 *Red Broken Mountainous Labyrinth*, 2008. Aluminum venetian blinds, powder-coated aluminum hanging structure, steel wire rope, moving spotlights, DMX controller, spotlights. 345 × 798 × 727 cm. Tanoto Family Collection. Installation view of *Haegue Yang: In the Cone of Uncertainty*, The Bass Museum of Art, Miami Beach, USA, 2019. Photo: Zachary Balber, The Bass Museum of Art.

11 *Rotating Notes*, 2010. Powder-coated steel sheet, ball bearings, magnets, notes. Five parts, 144 × 109 cm each. Courtesy of Galerie Barbara Wien, Berlin. Photo: Gwangju Biennale.

12 *Central Composition in Explosion – Trustworthy #184*, 2012–2013. Various security envelopes and graph paper on cardboard, framed. 11 parts, 98.2 × 98.2 cm or 68.2 × 68.2 cm. Installation view of *Family of Equivocations*, Aubette 1928 and Museum of Modern and Contemporary Art, Strasbourg, 2013. Photo: Mathieu Bertola, Musées de la Ville de Strasbourg.

13 *Munich Tilt*, 2000. Acrylic paint. 350 × 1600 cm. Black stripes tilted one degree. Installation view of *Café Helga & Galerie Goldankauf*, Kunstraum München, Munich, Germany, 2000.

14 *Shifted Tilt*, 2001. MDF, roof battens, acrylic paint. Dimensions variable. 5 black rectangles painted on specially constructed walls. Installation view of *1 Site – 2 Places*, Galerie der Stadt, Sindelfingen, Germany, 2001.

15 *Field of Teleportation*, 2011. In collaboration with Studio Manuel Raeder. Digital color print. Dimensions variable. Courtesy of Galerie Chantal Crousel, Paris and Kukje Gallery, Seoul. Installation view of *The Art and Technique of Folding the Land*, Aspen Art Museum, Colorado, USA, 2011. Photo: Jason Dewey.

16 *Seoul Guts – Medicine Man*, 2010. Clothing rack, casters, light bulbs, cable, zip ties, terminal strips, nylon cord, rope, metal chains, metal rings, bells, dried ginseng, dried garlic, pill boxes, plastic fruit, massage rollers, counter. 200 × 100 × 90 cm. Part of *Soul Guts*, 2010. Collection of Leeum Museum of Art. Installation view of *Voice over Three*, Artsonje Center, Seoul, South Korea, 2010. Photo: Kim Sang Tae.

17 *Female Natives*, 2010 and *Medicine Men*, 2010 (detail). Collection of National Museum of Contemporary Art, Korea and Zabludowicz Collection, respectively. Installation view of *The Great Acceleration*, Taipei Biennial 2014, Taiwan, 2014. Photo: Taipei Fine Arts Museum.

18 *The Intermediate – Lion Dance on One Leg*, 2015. Artificial straw, powder-coated steel frame, casters, plastic raffia string, knitting yarn, cord, Indian bells, Korean bridal crowns. 215 × 160 × 94 cm. Part of *The Intermediates – Dancing in Woven Masks*, 2015. Leo Shih Collection, Taichung. Installation view of *Shooting the Elephant 象 Thinking the Elephant*, Leeum Museum of Art, Seoul, South Korea, 2015. Photo: © Leeum Museum of Art.

19 *Brier Teardrop Formation – Mesmerizing Mesh #39*, 2021. *Hanji*, graph paper on alu-dibond, framed. 62 × 62 cm. Collection of Yeo Tae Hong, Busan.

20 *Spiritual-Powered Soul Stick – Mesmerizing Mesh #28*, 2021. *Hanji* on alu-dibond, framed. 62 × 42 cm. Collection of Wonkee Lee, Daegu.

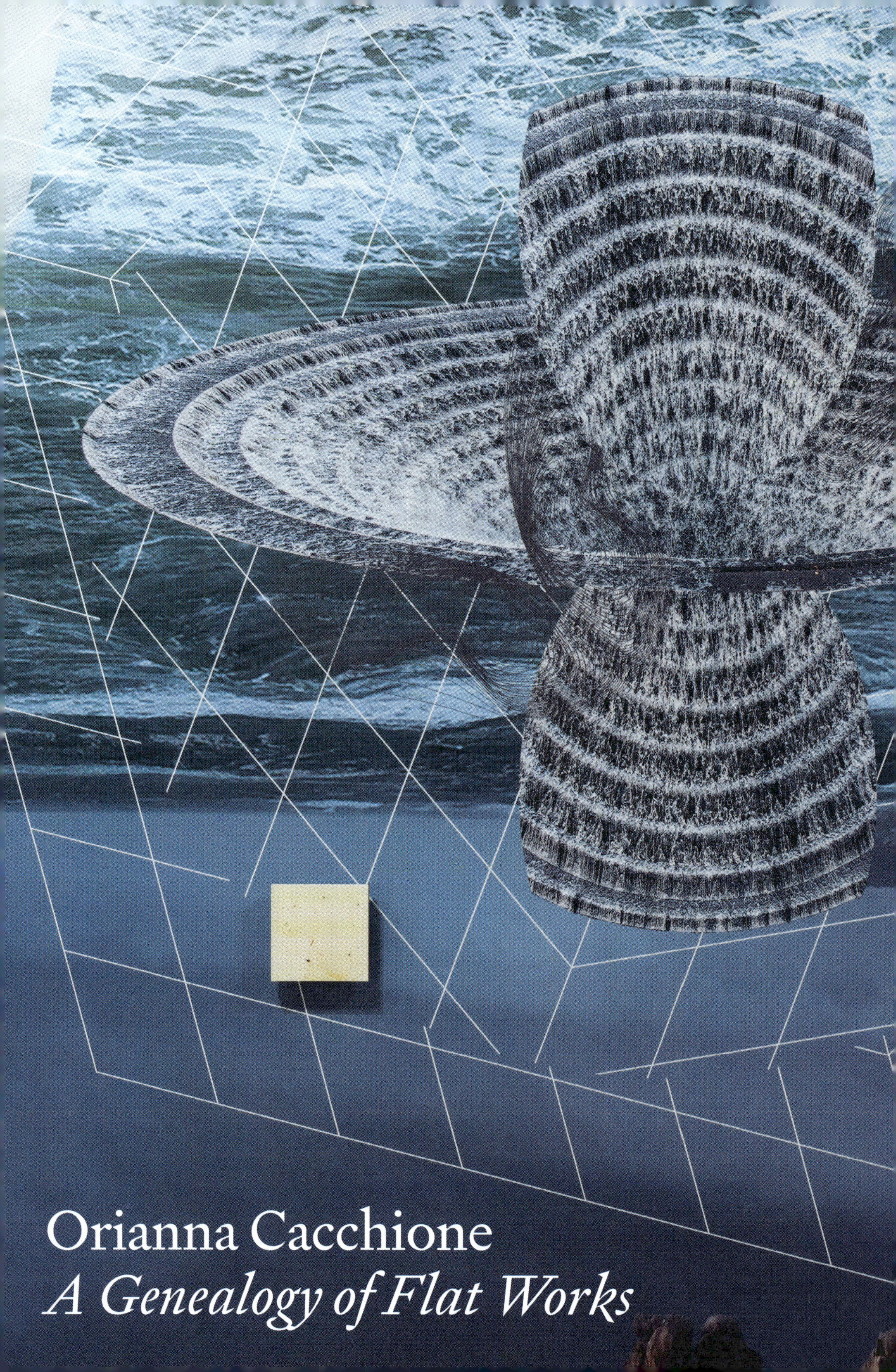

Orianna Cacchione
A Genealogy of Flat Works

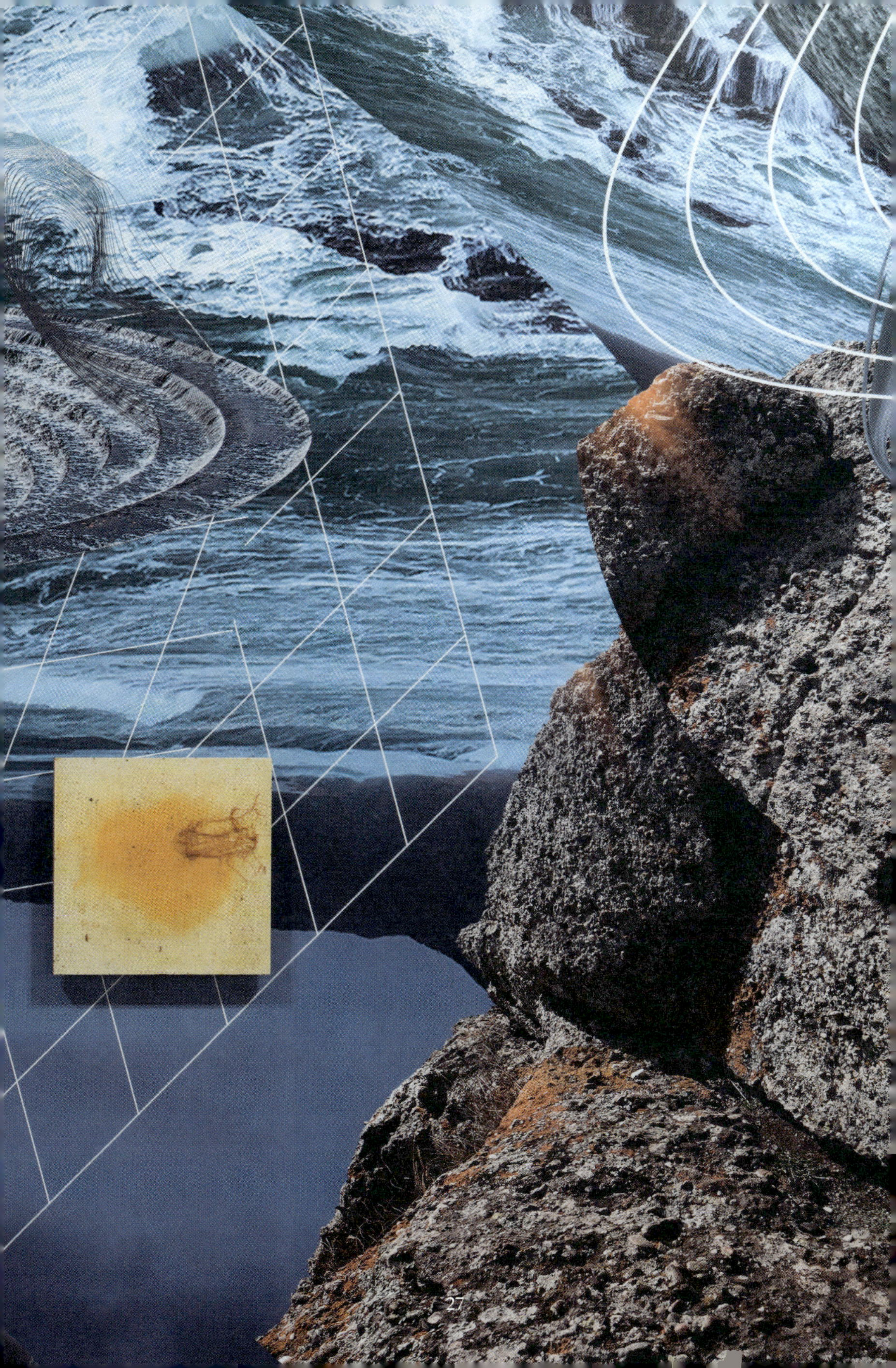

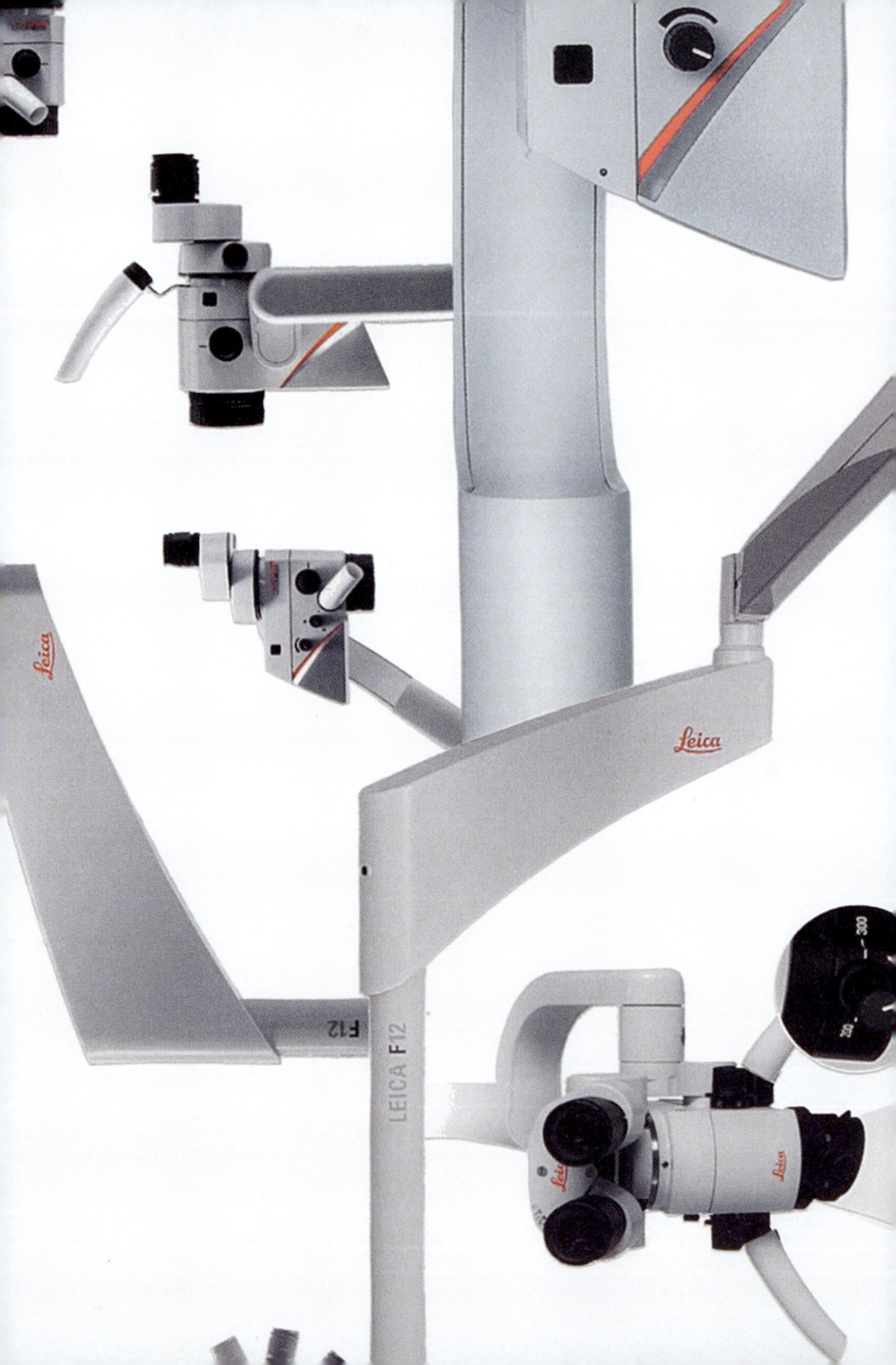

Hardware Store Collages 1994–2019

Haegue Yang began transforming cut-outs of the goods listed
on the pages of hardware store catalogues into rather small-sized
collages in 1994 when she first arrived in Germany to study
at the Städelschule in Frankfurt. At the time, she frequented
the *baumarkt* (hardware store); its highly organized rows of
abundantly available goods paralleled the orderly presentation
of wares in free catalogues ready to take home. The numerous
pages of indexed products seemed like a visual dictionary—
an act of translation as she learned not only German but
systems of production that could be at once appropriated
and deconstructed. Using a method of cutting, pasting and
rearranging, the *Hardware Store Collages* appropriate these
catalogues, reconfiguring their wares into spiraling arrangements
of multiplying objects in space. Household goods and building
supplies are whimsically dislodged from their original places
within the structure of the catalogue and arranged on the
indefinite space of a monochrome background, breaking down
systems of organization and product photography. By privileging
the mundane products anyone can purchase, Yang recuperates and
reappropriates the ways the highly industrialized world is accessed.

In *Hardware Store Collage – Bauhaus Kitchen Sinks #1* (2013) [Plate 3],
cut-out shapes of shining silver sinks pile on top of each against
the glossy golden backdrop of solid chromolux paper. The
superimposition of sinks on top of the photograph-like paper
background implores a comparing and contrasting of the different
models, yet to what end is unclear. In other works, devices, cords,
and appliances are anthropomorphized into robot-like figures,
like the storage boxes that suggest the dancing arms and legs of
an off-balance figure in *Hardware Store Collage – Schäfer Storage
Boxes #1* (2017) [Plate 13]. They are pinwheeled together, mirrored,
centered as if exploding off the page, like the office chairs in
Hardware Store Collage – Schäfer Office Chairs #1 (2015) [Plate 9].
Ultimately, they reconfigure and refract the humble objects into
dizzying configurations of accumulation.

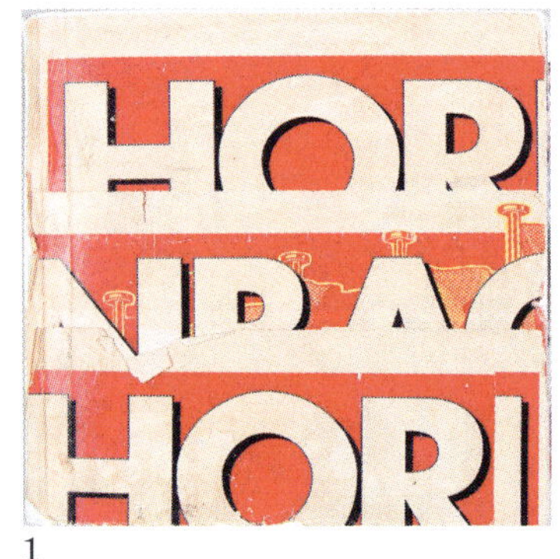

1

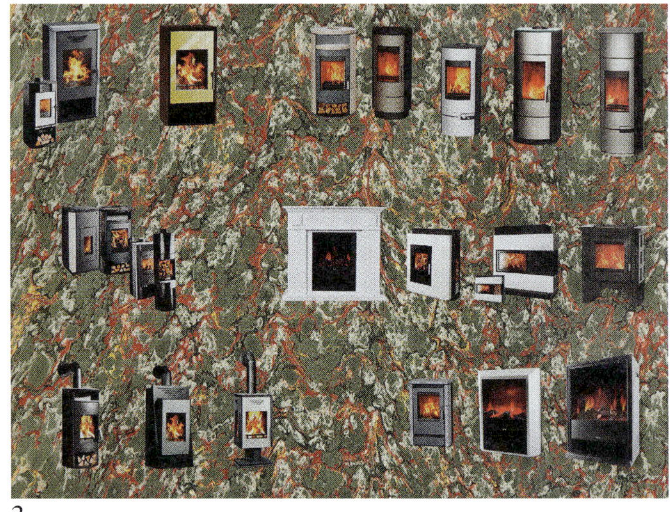

2

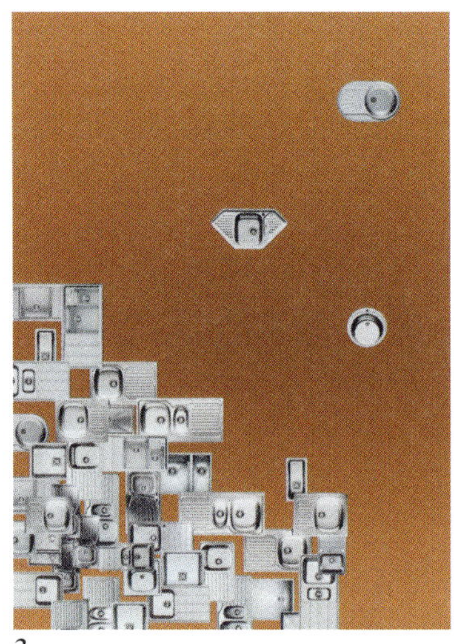

3

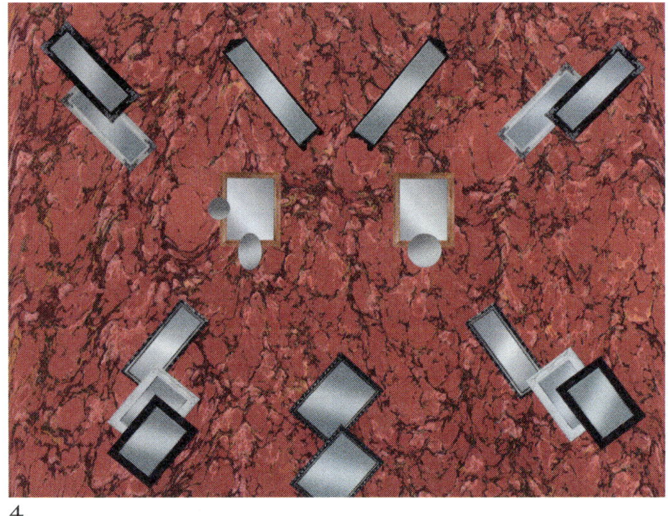

5

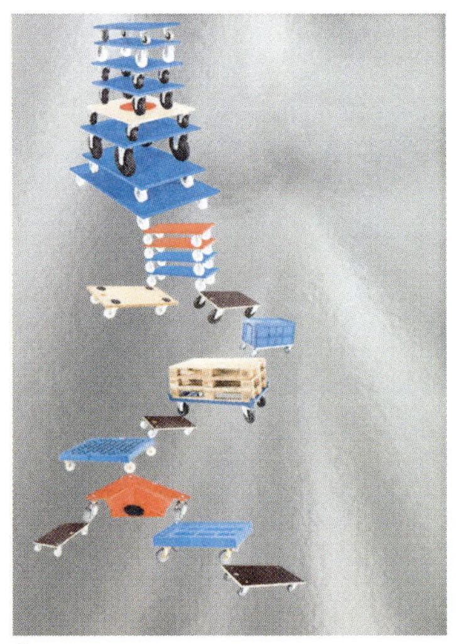

4

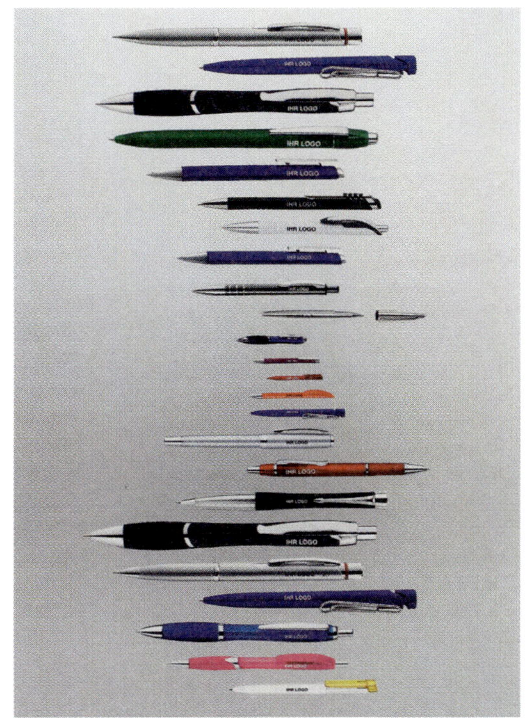

6

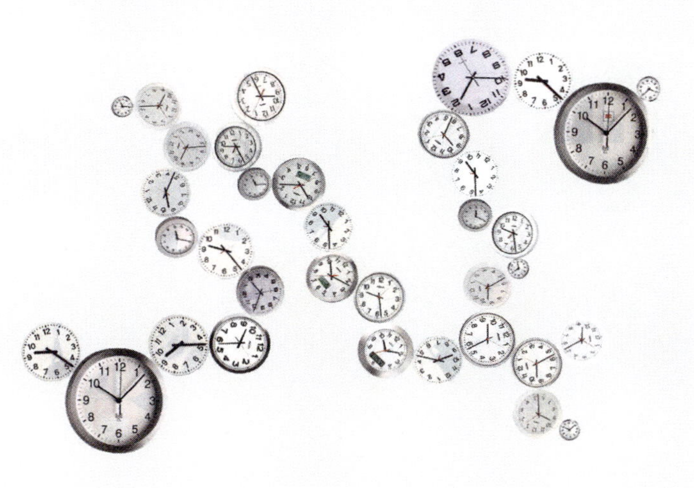

7

1   *Hornbachbuch*, 1994
2   *Hardware Store Collage –*
     Bauhaus Fire Places #1, 2013
3   *Hardware Store Collage –*
     Bauhaus Kitchen
     Sinks #1, 2013

4   *Hardware Store Collage –*
     Bauhaus Mirrors #1, 2013
5   *Hardware Store Collage –*
     Schäfer Furniture
     Dollies #1, 2014

6   *Hardware Store Collage –*
     Schäfer Ballpoints and
     Mechanical Pencils #1, 2015
7   *Hardware Store Collage –*
     Schäfer Wall Clocks #1, 2015

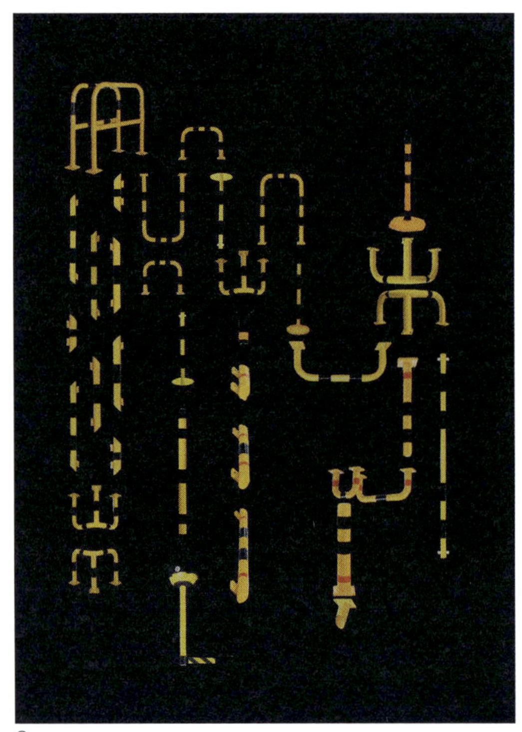

8

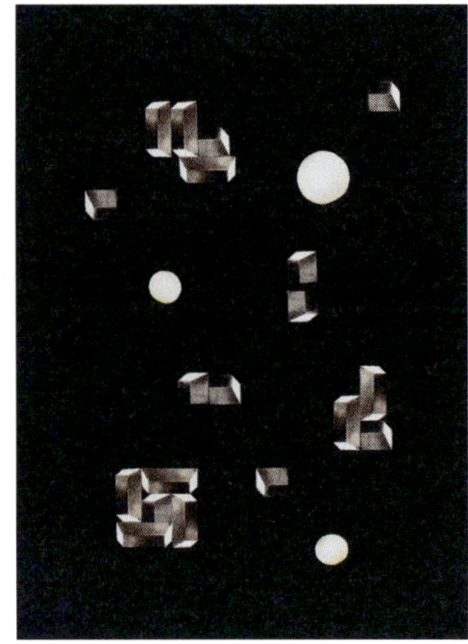

10

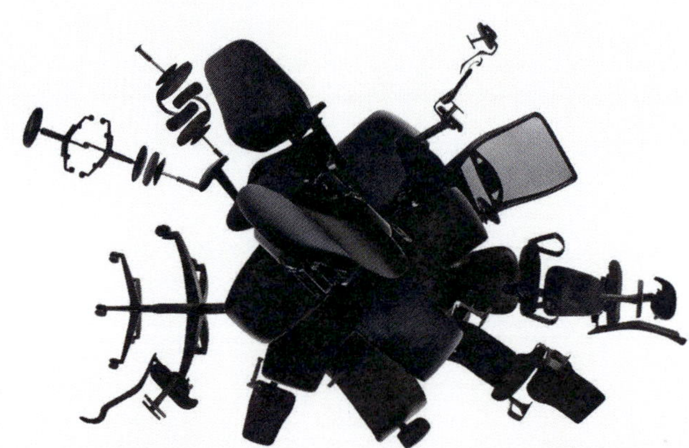

9

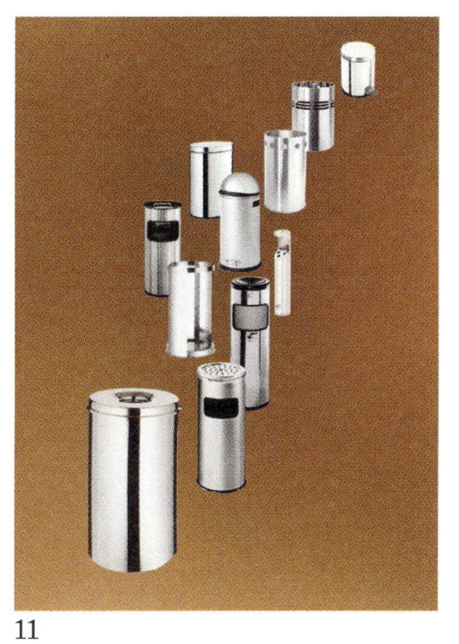

11

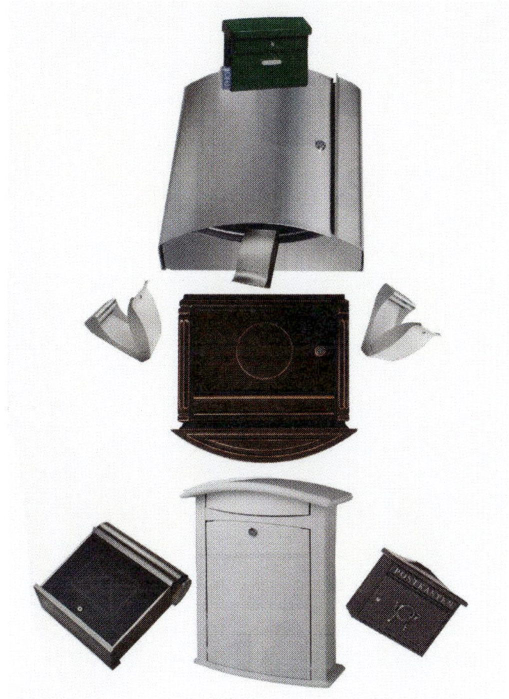

12

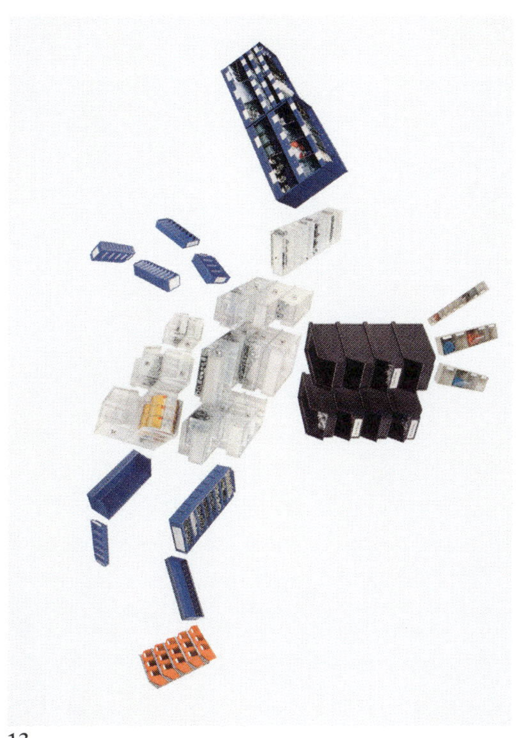

13

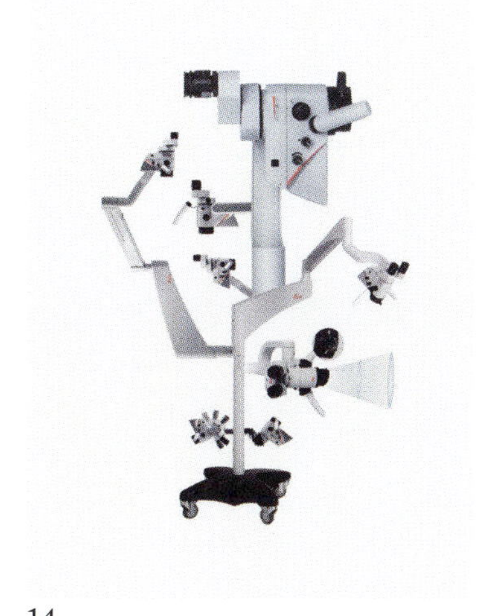

14

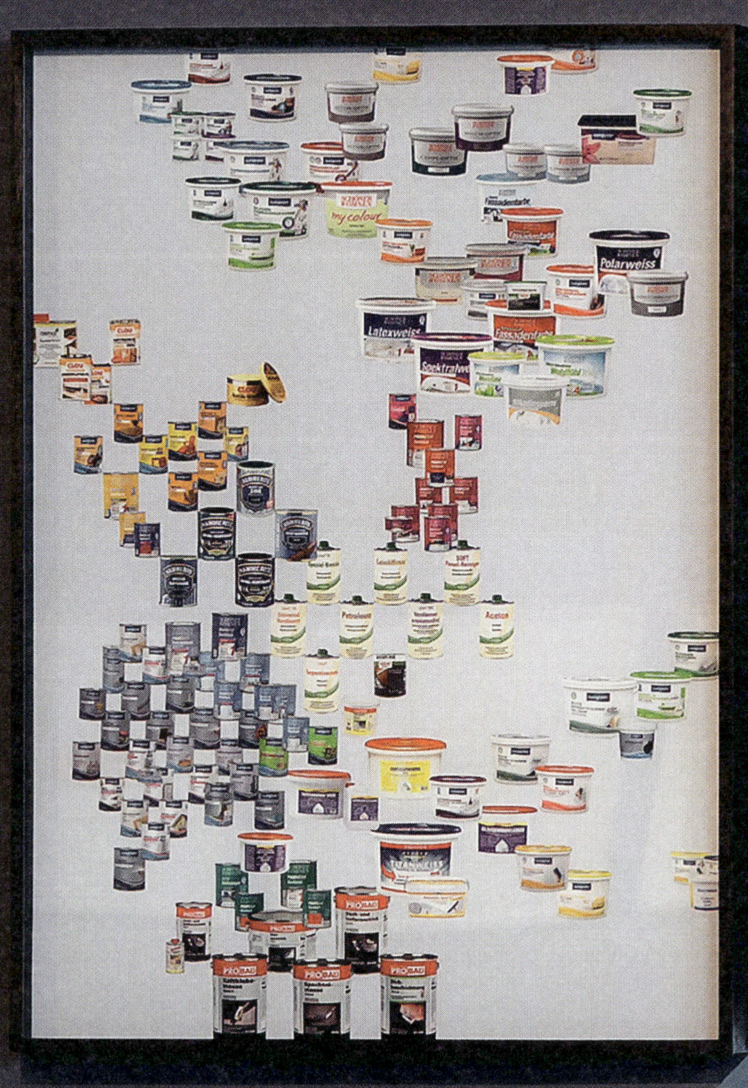

The Cone of Concern
Museum of Contemporary Art and Design (MCAD), Manila, Philippines, 2020

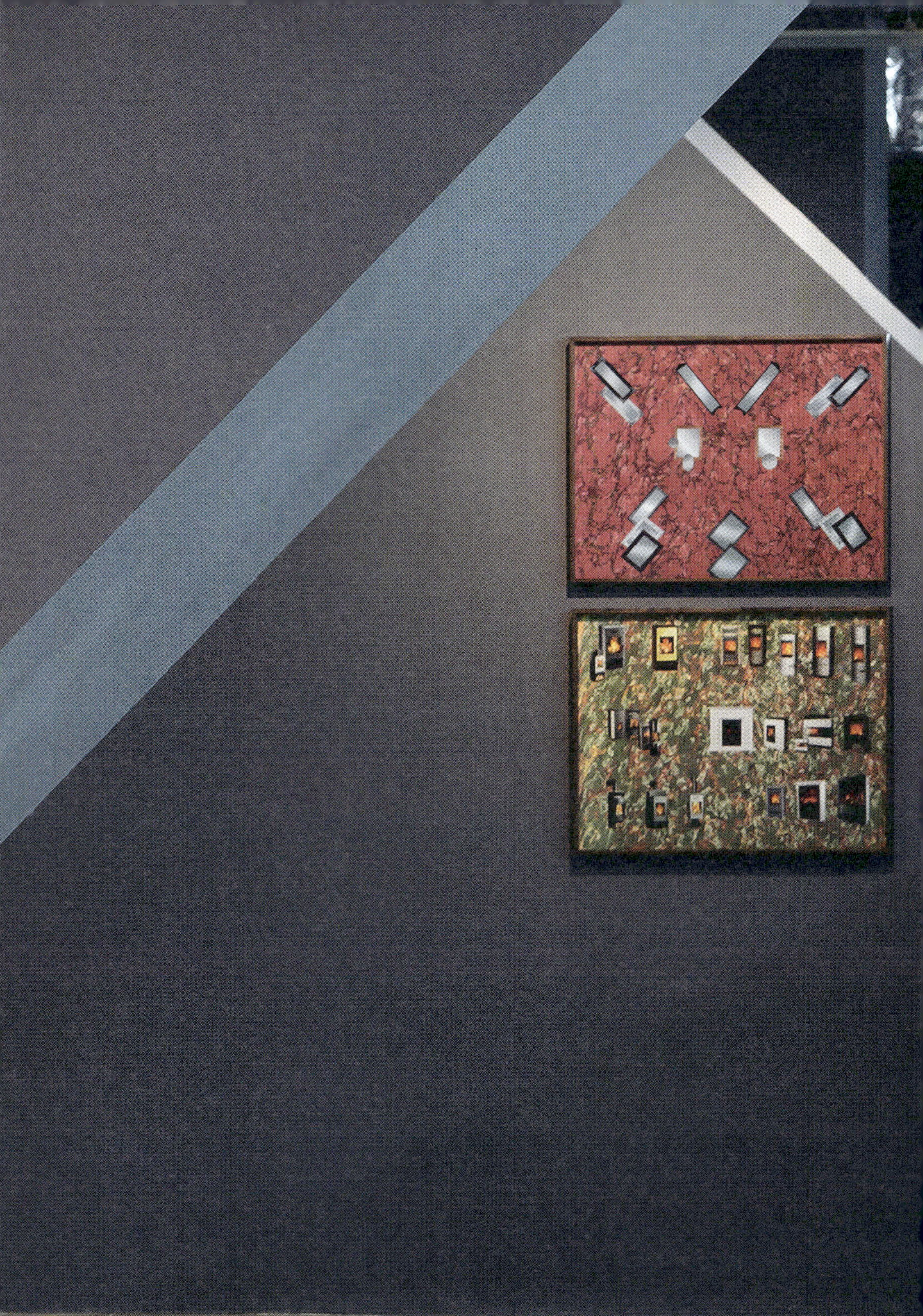

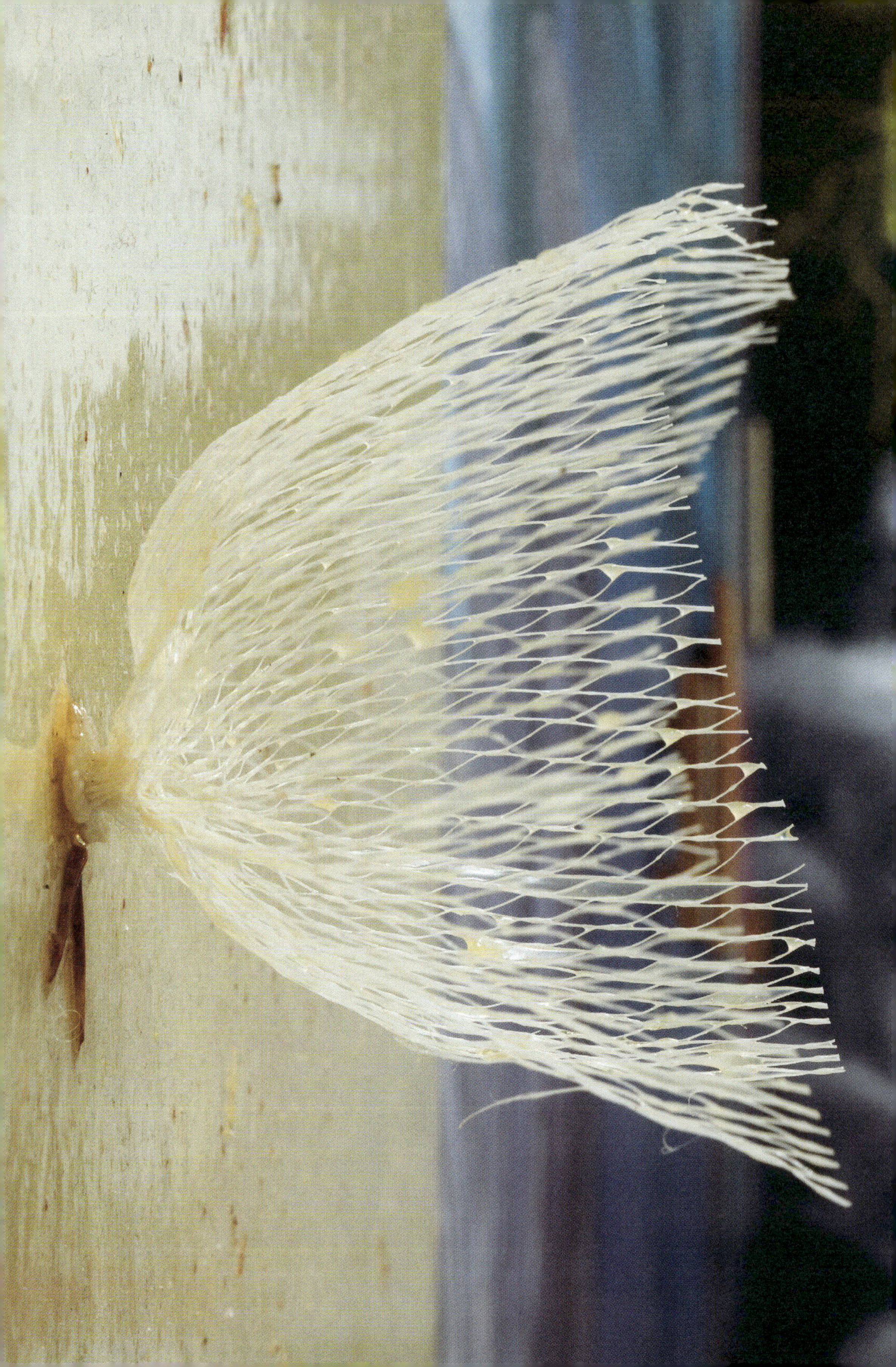

Lacquer Paintings since 1994

Like the *Hardware Store Collages*, the *Lacquer Paintings* date to Yang's arrival in Germany. Yang began experimenting with lacquer as a material, pouring the transparent lacquer paint onto scrap pieces of MDF sawn into rough grid patterns or variously covered with small objects. The cheap, common material acted not only as an antidote to more conventional methods of painting and later sculpture-making, but also as a subtle allusion to the long history of lacquerware in Asian art. Exchanging the expensive natural lacquer derived from tree sap with an artificial, industrial material becomes a mode of unlearning, and also a means to chronicle studio life. In the earliest of these paintings made between 1994 and 1996, the lacquer encased small drawings, wisps of thread and needles, fishing hooks and dust, testing how the remnants of Yang's studio practice in their simplest form can be preserved, fossilized. Returning briefly to the series in 2000, Yang covered arrangements of graph paper, photocopies, and photographs saturating the thin paper to create a transparency beyond standard collages. In 2011 Yang resumed the series, capturing both the ephemeral and material traces of her time in the studio. Lacquer engulfs the cut-offs and cast-aways left behind while making other artworks—like the orderly lines of electric crimps and terminals in *Unknown Schema* (2019) [Plate 19] as well the produce grown in her studio garden. At the same time, the paintings, like *Midsummer Dust, Dirt, and Grit in the Breeze of Saché* (2015–2017) [Plate 16], are left outside to dry, exposed to rain, and catching dust, insects, and other particles blown across their surfaces. Shifting between organic, chance compositions, and rigid organizations, the *Lacquer Paintings* continuously emphasize their own poor materiality *à la* Arte Povera, and index the studio conditions of their own making.

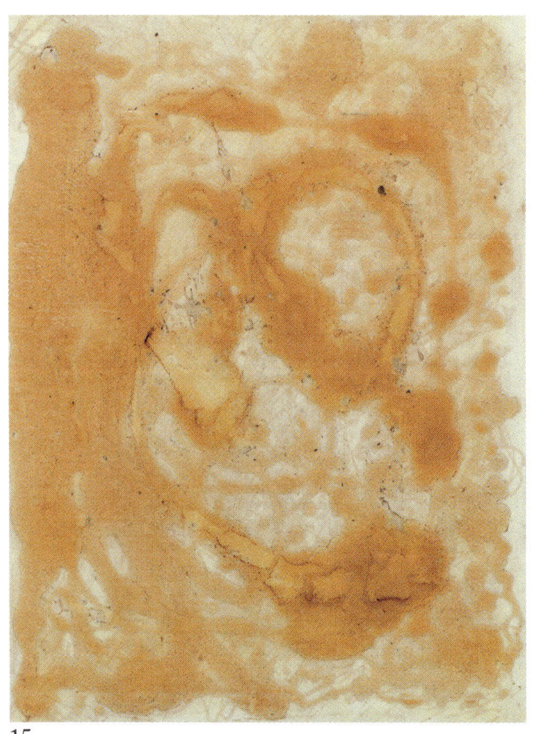

15

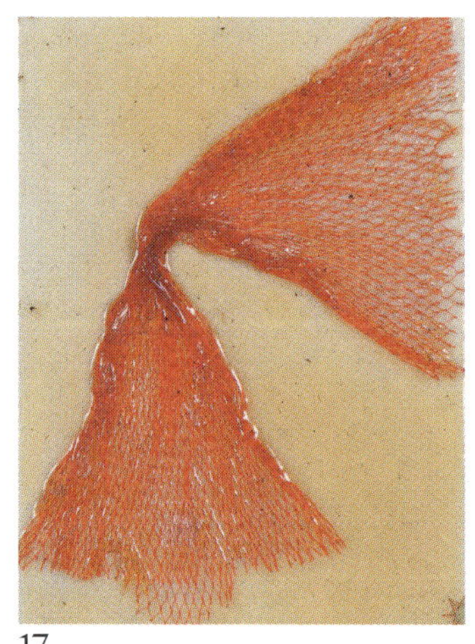

17

16

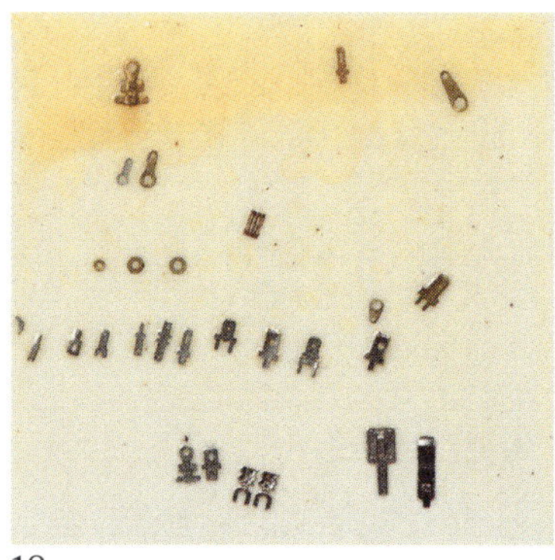

18

19

20

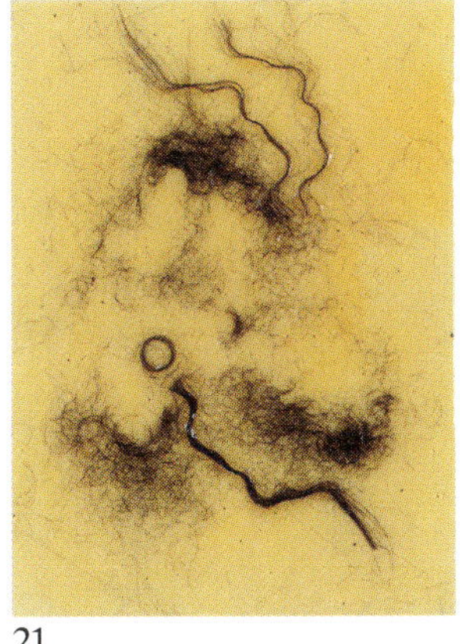

21   22

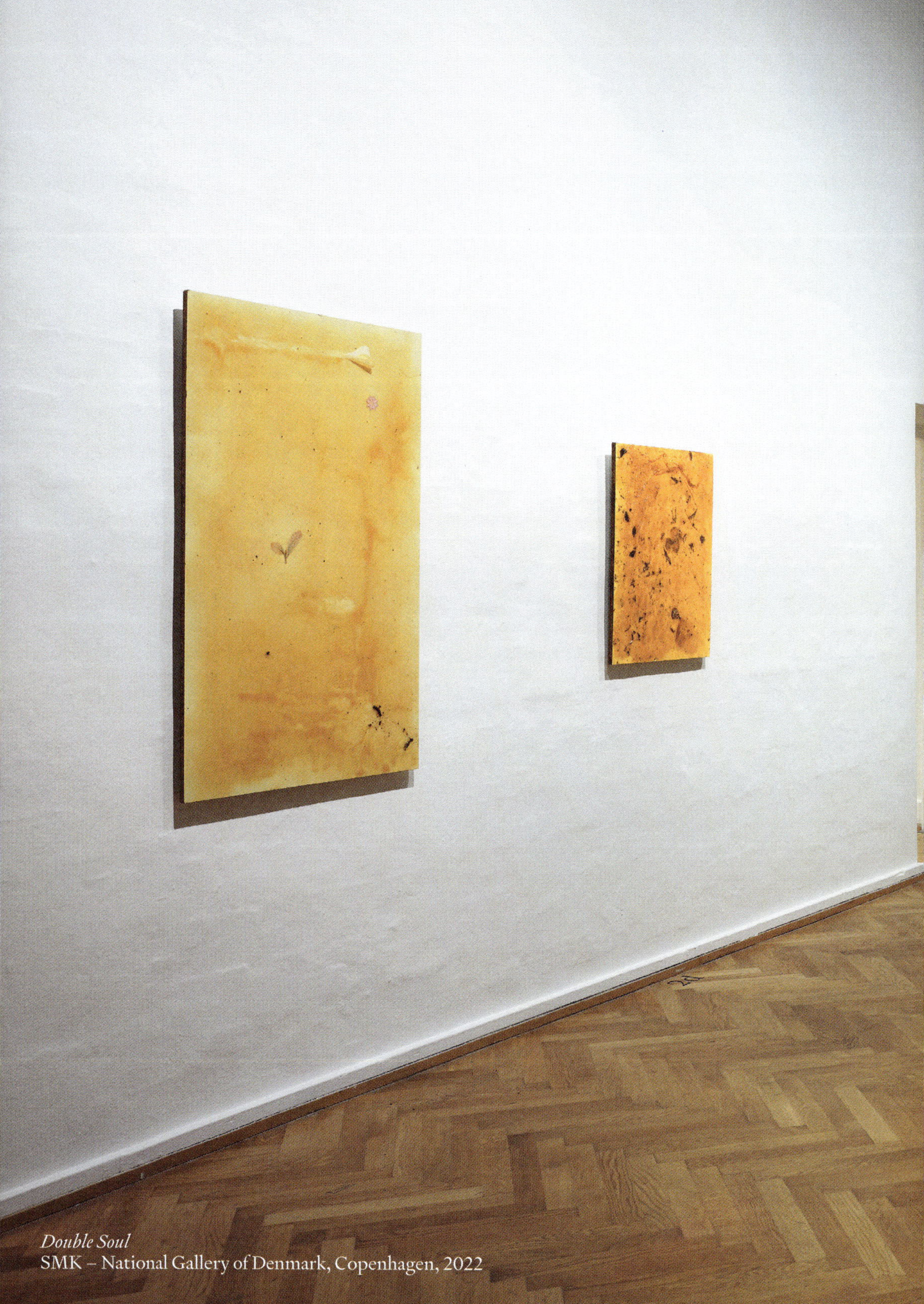

Double Soul
SMK – National Gallery of Denmark, Copenhagen, 2022

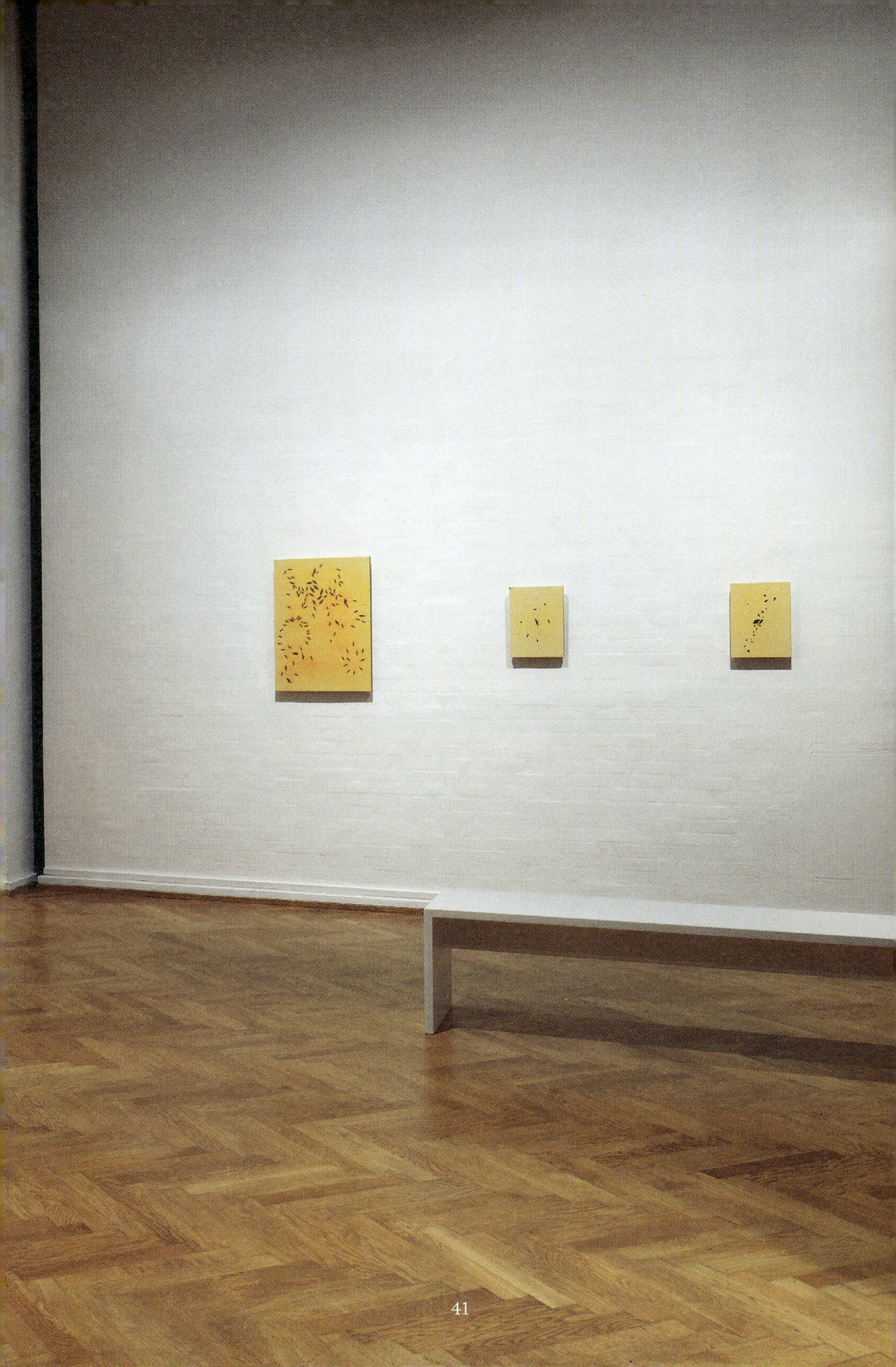

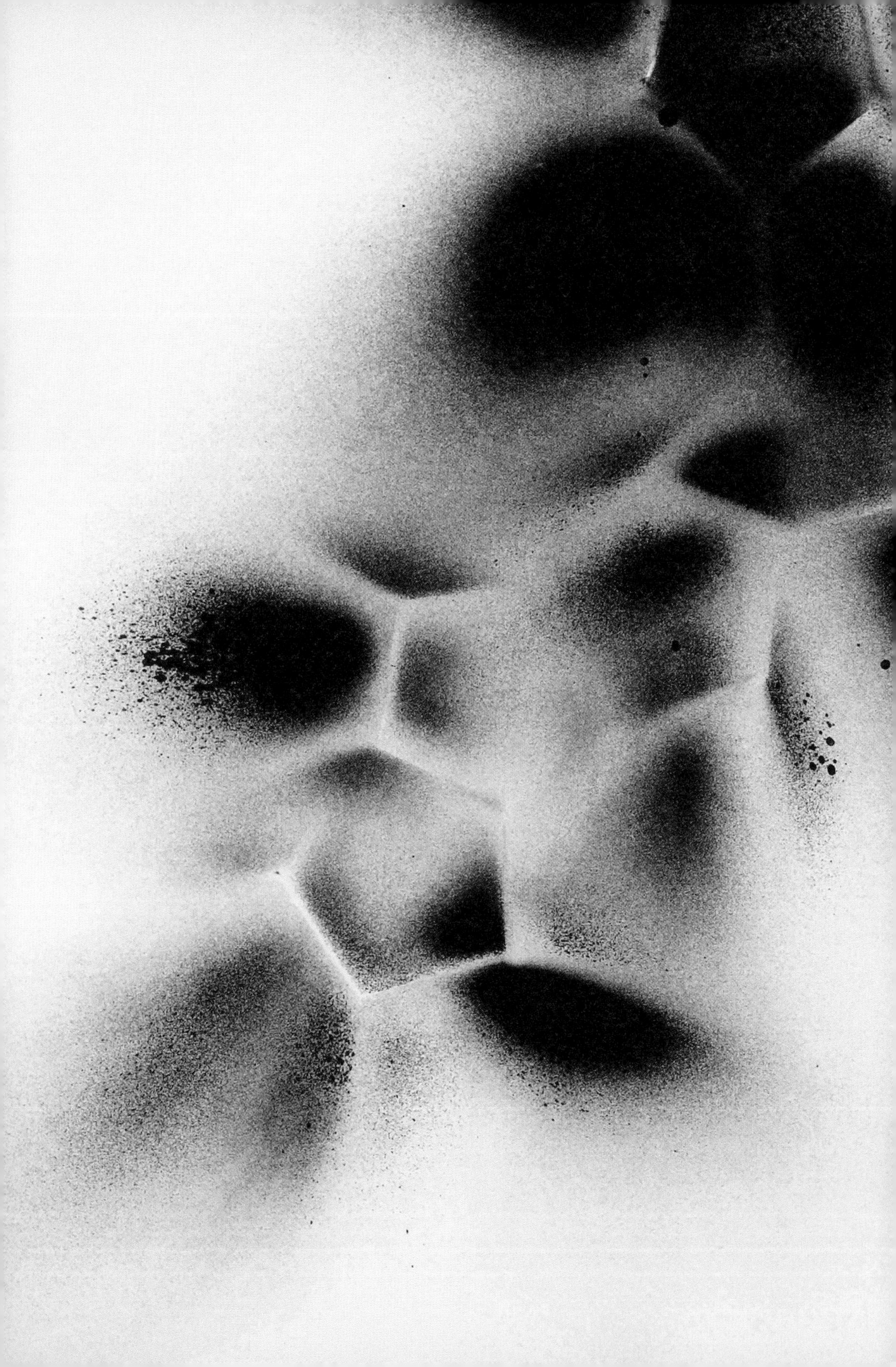

Non-Foldings 2007–2015

The *Non-Folding* series documents and arranges abstract origami polyhedrons through the registers of absence, negative space, and flattening. Yang uses black, white, and silver spray paint to hazily record the edges and volumes of the multi-faceted shapes, leaving only the shadows of the shapes on a large sheet from a paper roll. Some index patterns of different shapes, while others create explosion-like halos of black around each object, and still another type captures the tipping of a single shape across the flat surface of the paper like *Non-Folding – Geometric Tipping #15* (2013) [Plate 23]. Later, Yang began crushing the stained origami shapes and arranging them into constellations as demonstrated in *Non-Folding – Scenarios of Non-Geometric Folding #15* (2015) [Plate 26].

While first titled *Non-Folding* in 2007, Yang began working with origami, its traces, reproductions, and destruction much earlier. Throughout 2004 a group of origami objects appeared in various forms and registers in different artworks: as props in the video work, *Unfolding Places* (2004); as shadows left in spray-paint in the flat work, *Cove* (2004); as sculptural objects in the installation, *Origami Dust* (2004/2012); and eventually as photographs in *Last Destination Brussels* (2004) [Plate 53]. Two years later, origami objects were prominently placed in the immersive installation, *Sadong 30* (2006), where Yang began to understand origami as both object and conceptual modality. These different incarnations of origami shapes suggest the importance not only of the objects themselves, but also of the strategy of folding itself. The careful transformation of flat paper into three-dimensional objects through the simplicity of folding becomes a manifestation of moving in time and space. In the *Non-Foldings*, instead of creating volume, Yang compresses it, flattening the original origami objects through both physical and metaphorical means, ultimately abstracting objects in space.

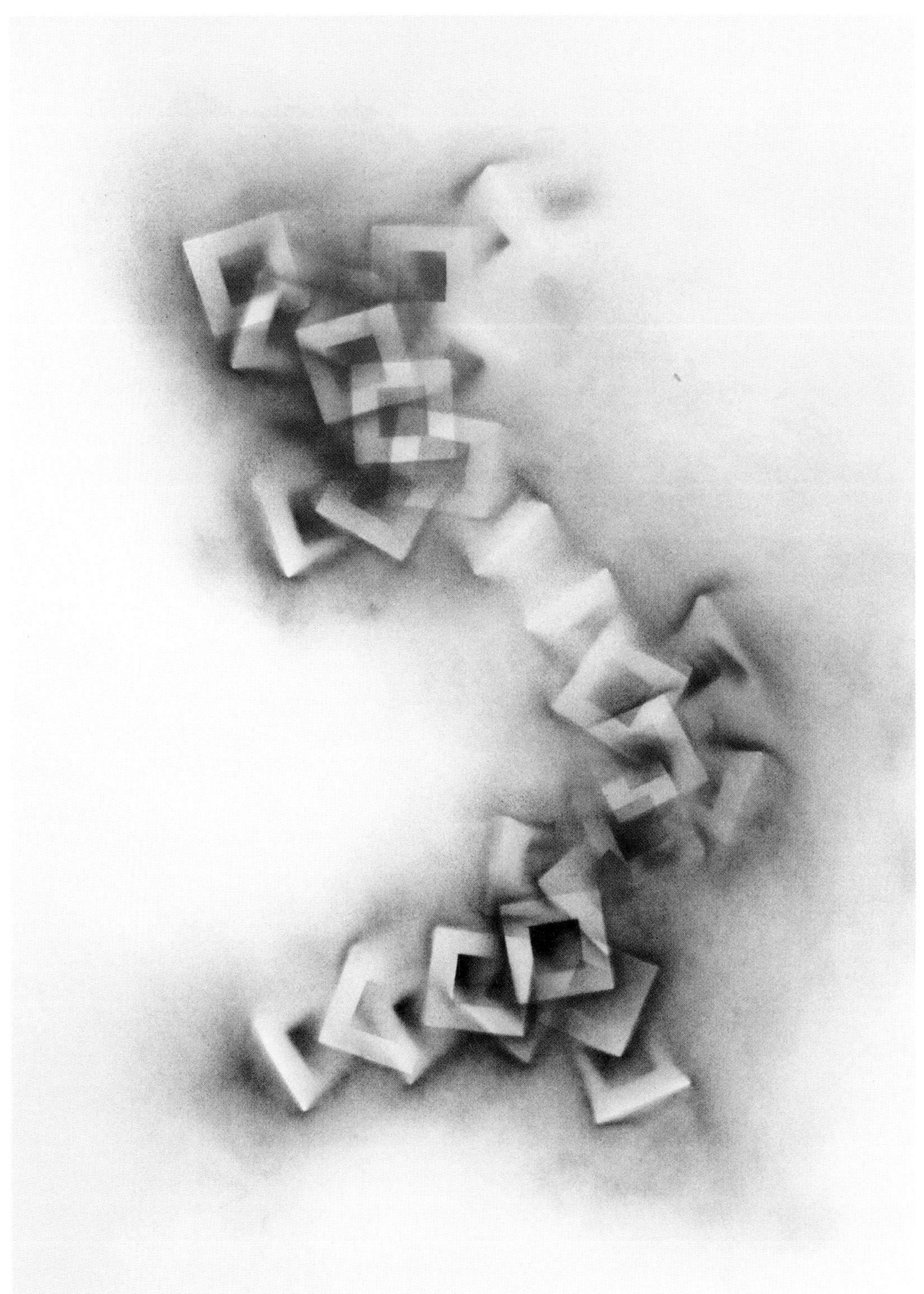

23

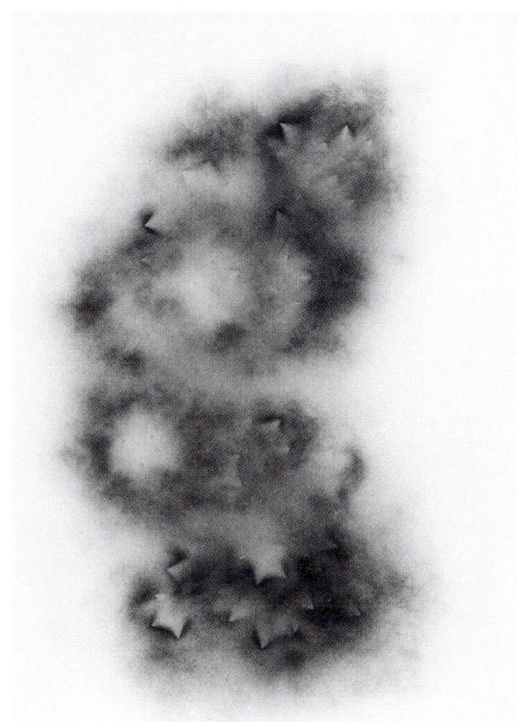

24

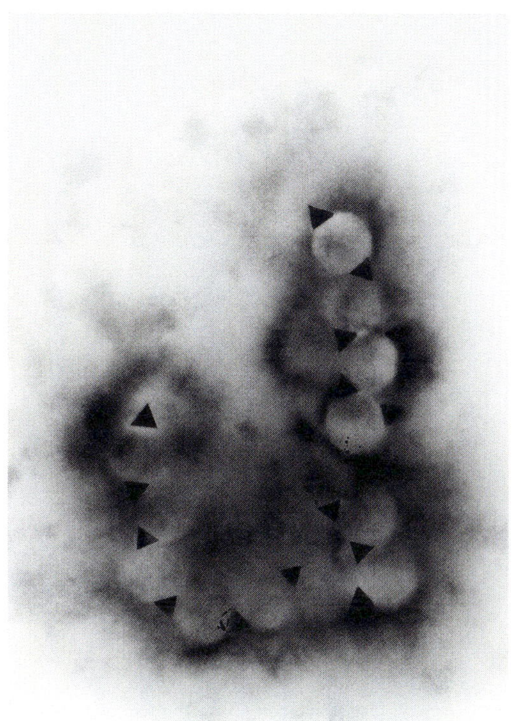

25

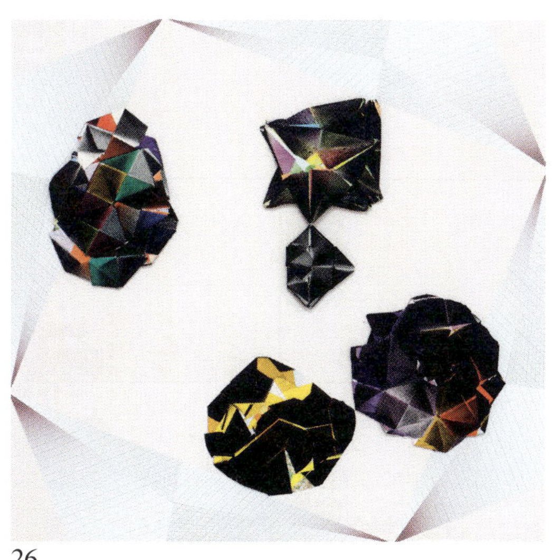

26

23 *Non-Folding – Geometric Tipping #15*, 2013
24 *Non-Folding – Geometric Tipping #59*, 2015

25 *Non-Folding – Geometric Tipping #65*, 2015

26 *Non-Folding – Scenarios of Non-Geometric Folding #15*, 2015

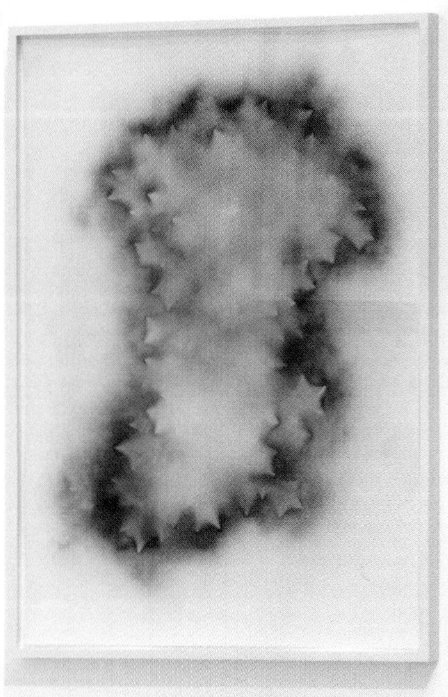
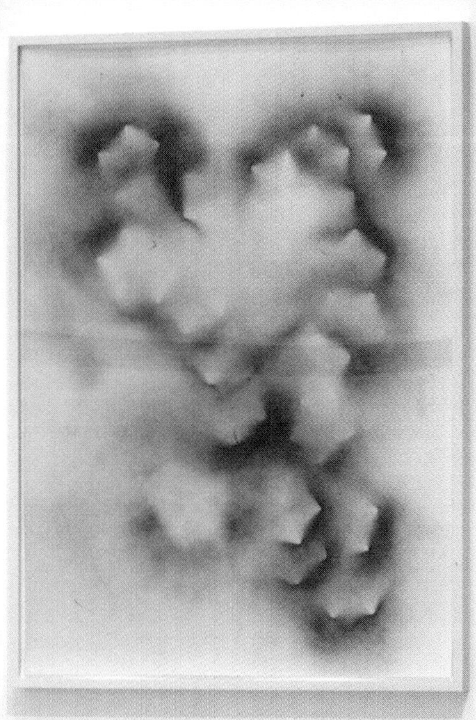

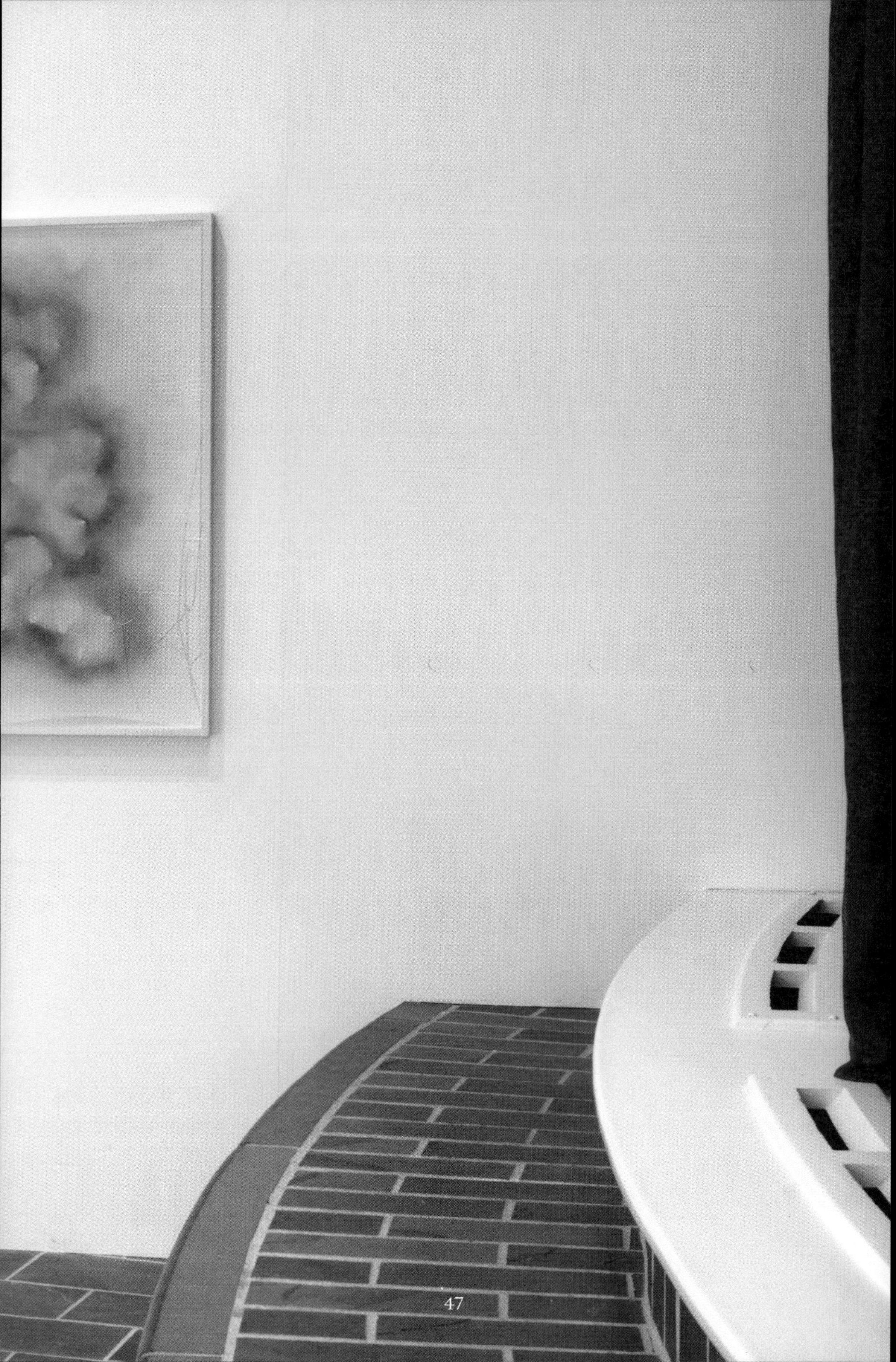

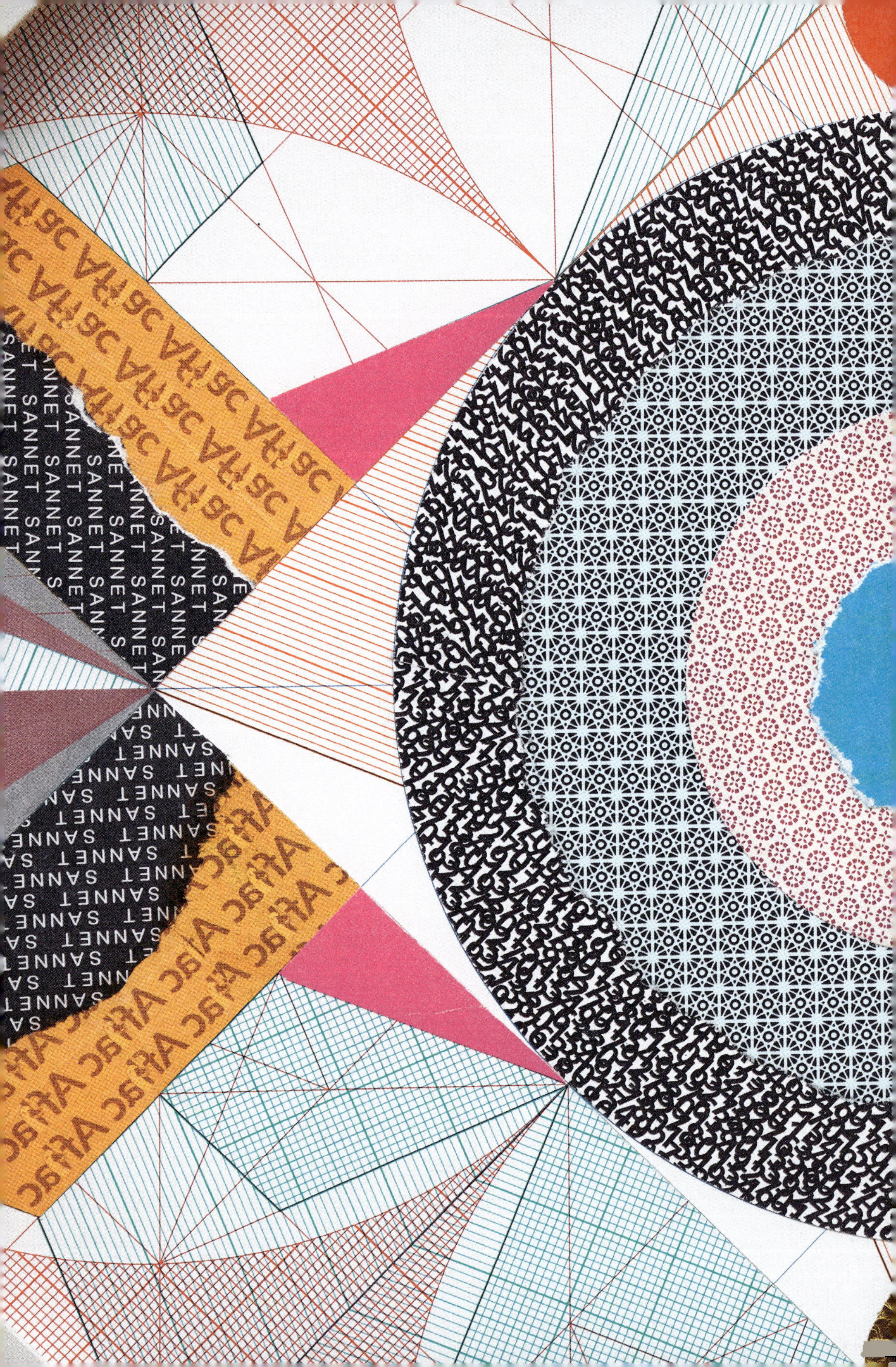

SANNET

Trustworthies 2010–2020

First started in 2010 and counting more than 300 individual artworks, the *Trustworthies* are by far the most prolific series Yang has undertaken. The *Trustworthies* are collages composed with the printed patterns on the inside of security envelopes and *Grid Bloc*, Yang's self-published graph paper. The earliest are fully abstract, minimalistic with gradients of color formed by small strips torn from the envelopes and arranged in orderly lines, falling like waves [Plate 27], turning at skewed angles, or rotating in space as if pinwheels [Plate 28]. Expanding beyond a single frame, many of the *Trustworthies* are repeated and arranged to design entire walls. Enveloping the gallery, they play with space and interiority, real and virtual.

Seemingly the most abstract of all of Yang artworks, the *Trustworthies* almost too easily reveal their real-world referent. Look close enough, the tiny repeating letters spelling out Prudential, Credit Suisse, Central Finance, CitiBank come into focus and furtively evoke systems of international banking or data security. In Yang's choice of name for the series, she evokes the question of what makes someone, something, some artwork, some institution trustworthy? This line of questioning—how data is protected and by whom—is reinforced in *Certificate #1* (2010) [Plate 55] in which Yang discloses her own personal information, but only to the collector once the artwork is purchased. This contract between buyer and seller, collector and artist introduces new and in fact legally questionable forms of trust into the transaction. Here the dichotomy between securing and revealing personal information reaches a fever pitch and anticipates the strange communities built by social media—those that feign the presentation of an authentic self and those that crave an impossible privacy.

In the more recent *Trustworthies*, Yang incorporates strategies from the *Hardware Store Collages*, cutting out motifs from supermarket flyers to medical supply brochures and arranging them on top of the dizzying designs. In *Scanning Hot Inner Values – Trustworthy #378* (2019) [Plate 30], a sweet potato is ringed by an MRI machine and a glazed donut loops around a robotic arm.

The unexpected combinations of images parallel their koan-like titles, implying a need to reconcile the title with the collaged motifs, further abstracting the separation between daily life and technological advances. This duality exposes and glues together what Yang calls a "social segregation" between the low-cost grocery store goods and high-end technological products, only accessible for a certain milieu of specialists.

27

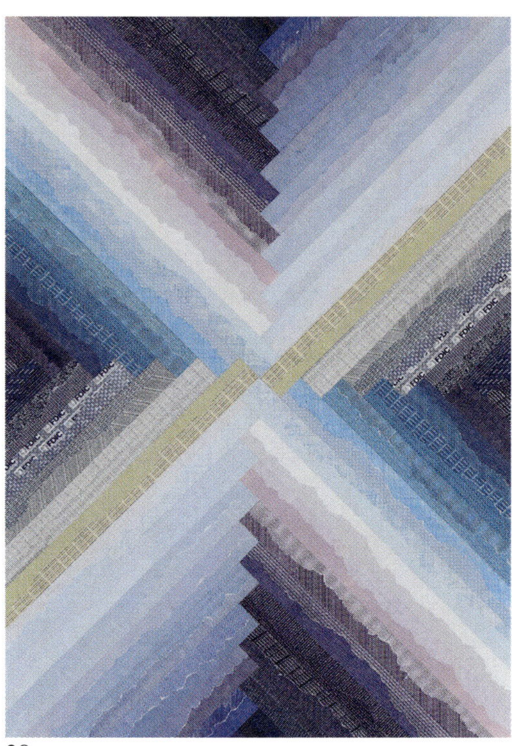

28

29

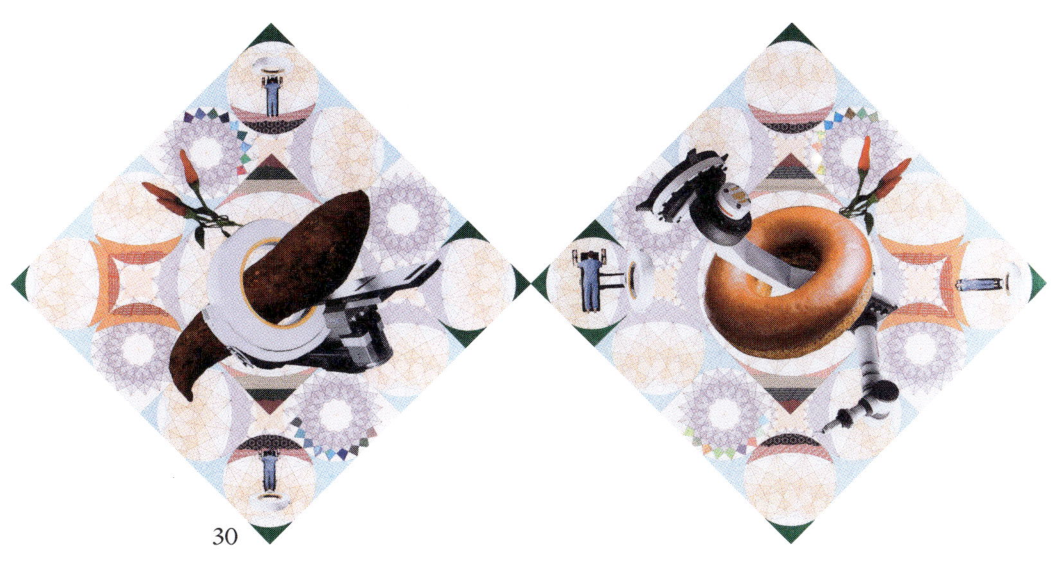

30

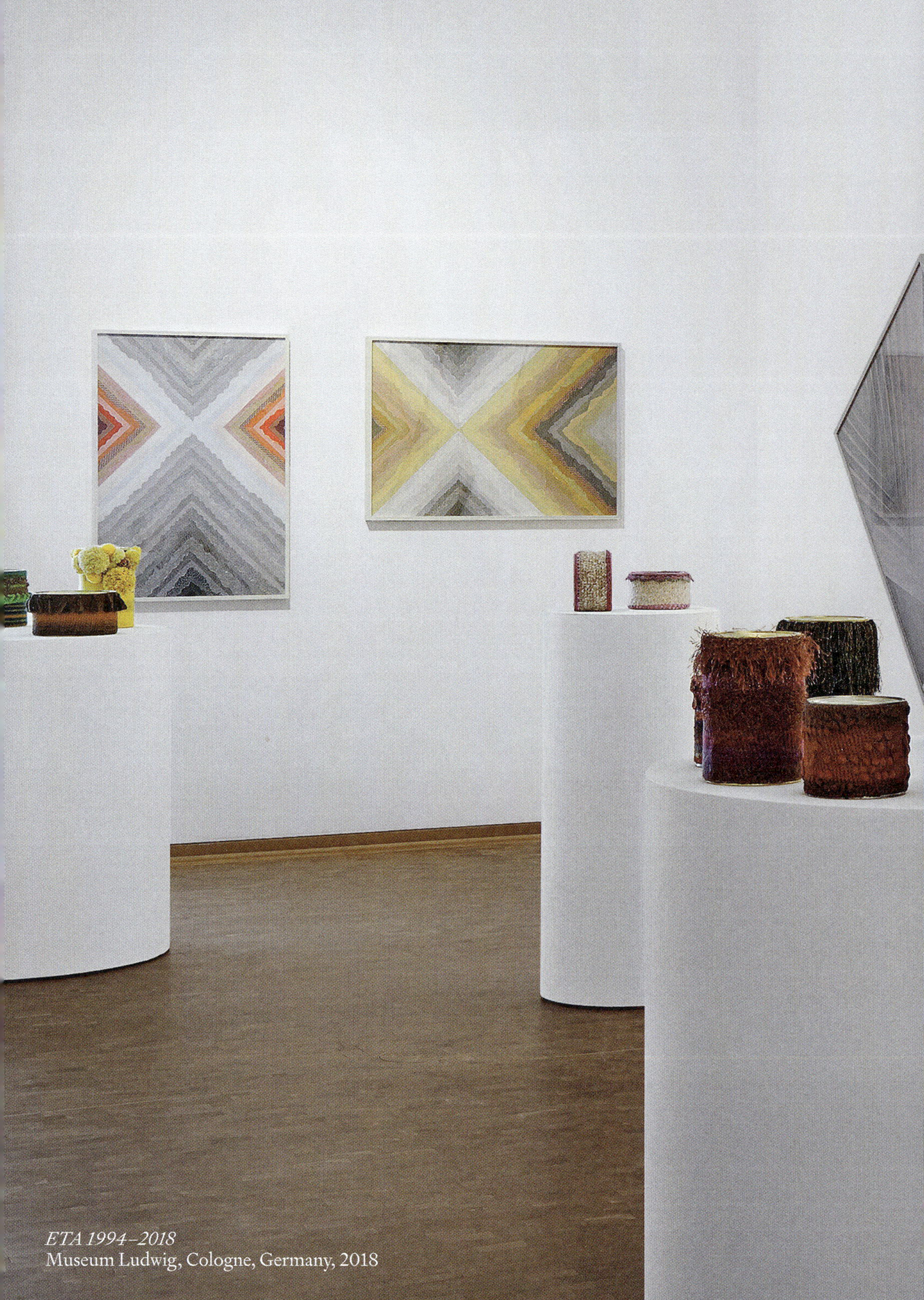

ETA 1994–2018
Museum Ludwig, Cologne, Germany, 2018

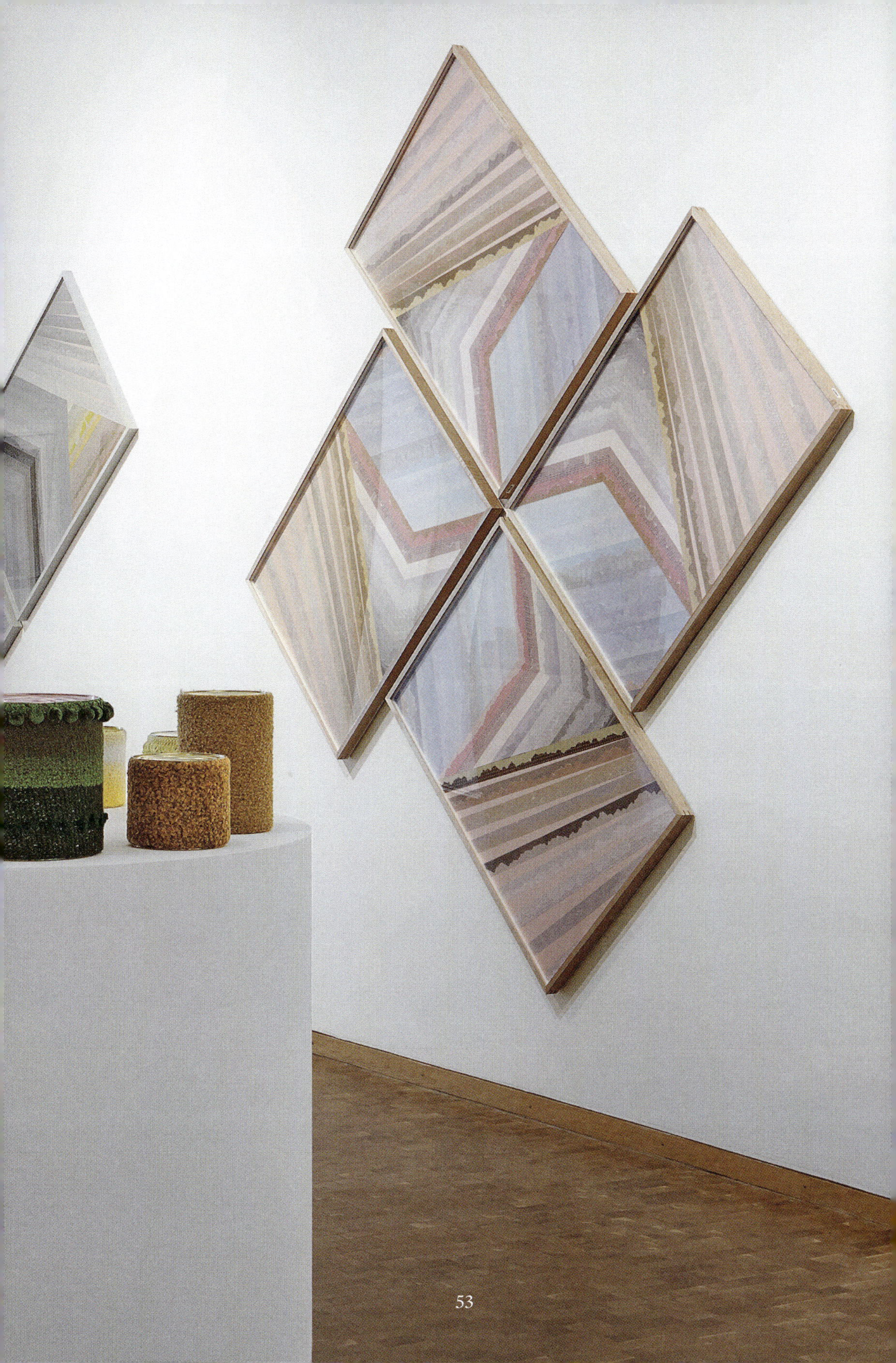

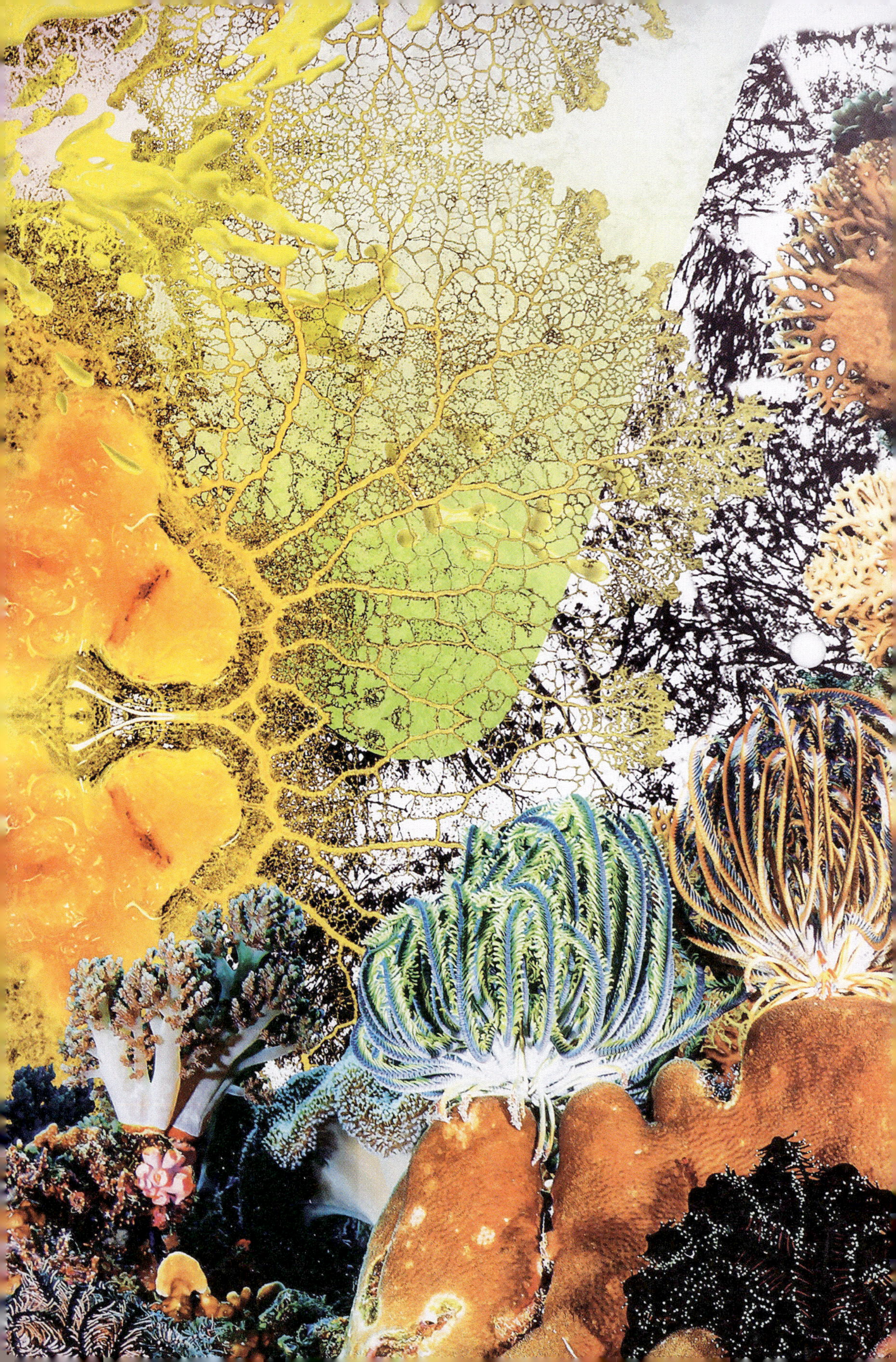

Wallpapers since 2011

Started just a year after the *Trustworthies*, Yang has so far created thirteen wallpapers, producing immersive environments that break through the confines of the white cube of the gallery. The earliest wallpaper installations, in fact the first three pieces, were exceedingly self-referential, photographs of Yang's previous artworks were collaged on top of indistinct backgrounds and cityscapes. Backdrops to both sculptures and flat works on view, the wallpapers reorder the hierarchy between scale and significance, as well as the artwork itself and its reproduction, compressing and consolidating real artworks and their images. Panoramic designs are created through multiplying geometries like the patterned designs of the *Trustworthies*.

As the wallpapers become more research-based, each wallpaper becomes an occasion to study a foreign environment, address local narratives and circumstances—including industrial or colonial histories, pagan traditions, or climate conditions—and realize its own whimsical perspective. In *Incubation and Exhaustion* (2018), medical machines and devices, surgical robots, and electronics are repeated in arrangements that evoke the *Hardware Store Collages* to address industries found in Montpellier, France, where the wallpaper was first commissioned. These are accompanied by flames, spices, chillies, garlic, and onions, that proliferate in dense groups according to the Occitane pagan rituals of the region. As demonstrated in *The Fantastic Warp and Weft of a Tropical Depression* (2020) [Page 57], *Non-Linear and Non-Periodic Dynamics* (2020) [Pages 26–27], and *Coordinates of Speculative Solidarity* (2019), weather events and climatic phenomenon are increasingly incorporated—saturated and modified photographic images including lightning bolts, crashing waves, pooling water, and burning fires as well as various open source 3D digital modelings of meteorological tools and devices. These diasporic relations of images, artworks, and natural formations are turned upside-down, repeated, mirrored, and unmoored from gravity, perspective, and violate any sense of chronological or spatial order.

Immersive and atmospheric, the wallpapers take on planetary transitions, most notably climate change. Installed on the glass wall enclosing the Mies van der Rohe staircase at the Arts Club of Chicago, *Incantations – Entwinement, Endurance, and Extinction* (2022) ^{Plate 31} was commissioned for the group exhibition with three chapters, *PLANET B. Climate Change and the New Sublime* and premiered in Venice in 2022. The imagery for *Incantations* departs from a view of mankind in a deep forest, where the pale sky appears between thick tree-trunks, yet continues with flattened, concentrated visual references to shamanistic paper objects, strands of DNA, graphs of photosynthesis, magic eyes, bells, tree branches, and coral reefs. Considered collectively, the wallpaper weaves together these dizzying and disparate references into a form of research into the as-yet-unknown breaking down scientific rationalism to suggest other forms of knowing and being.

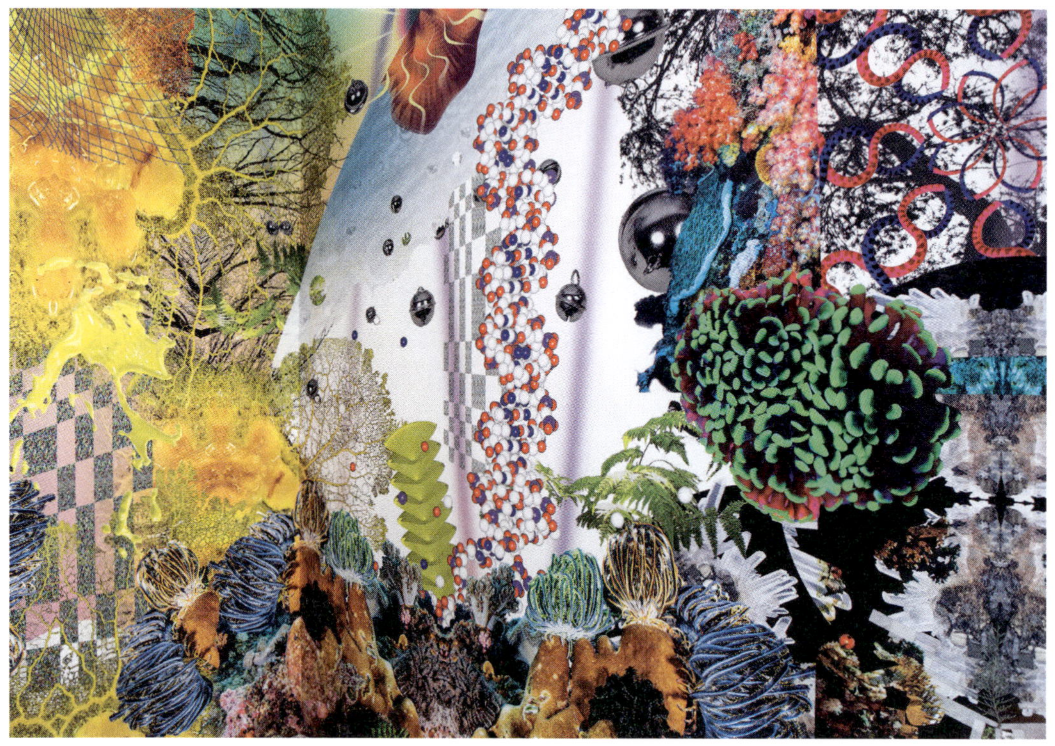

31 *Incantations – Entwinement,*
    Endurance, and Extinction, 2022

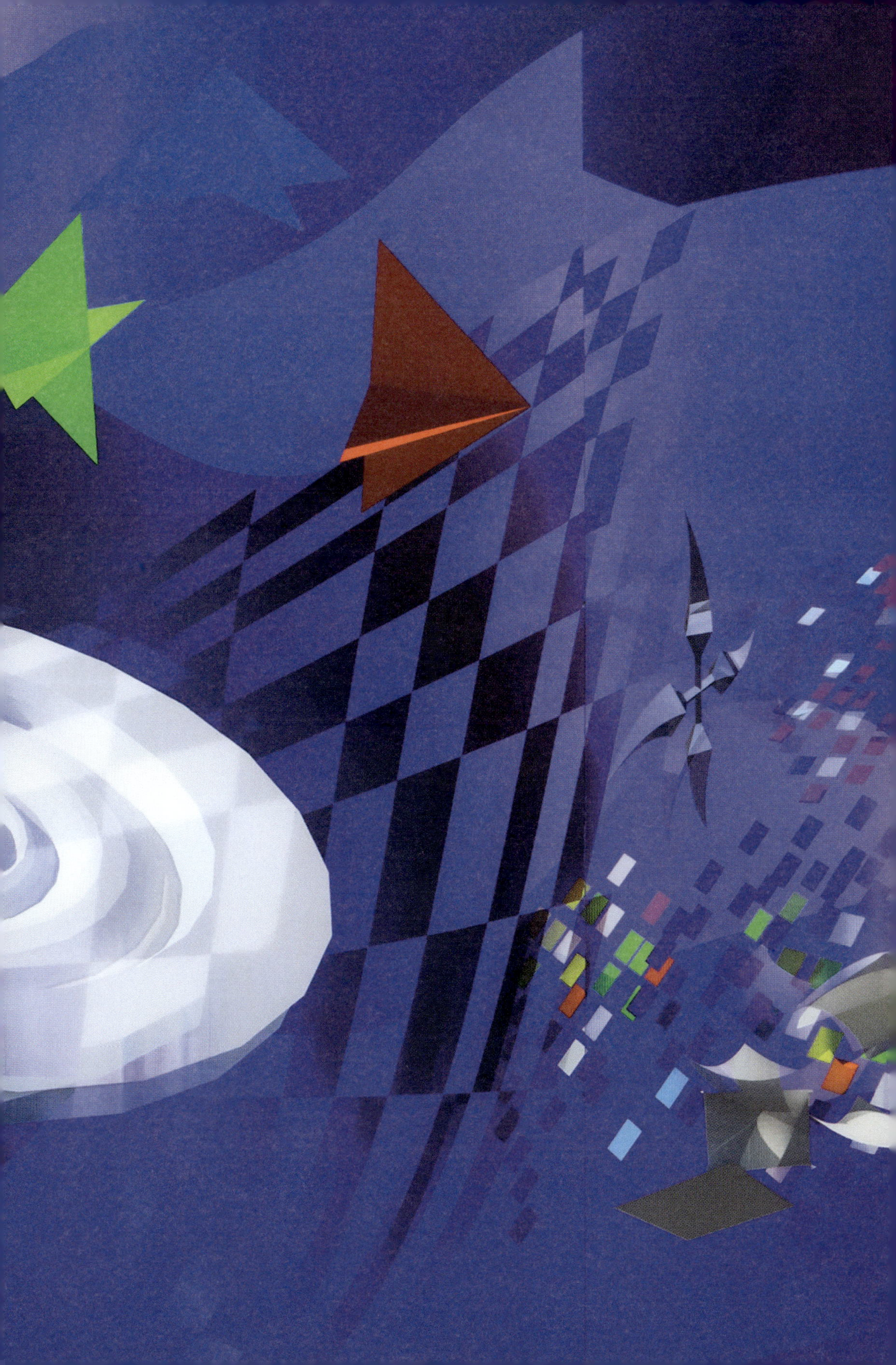

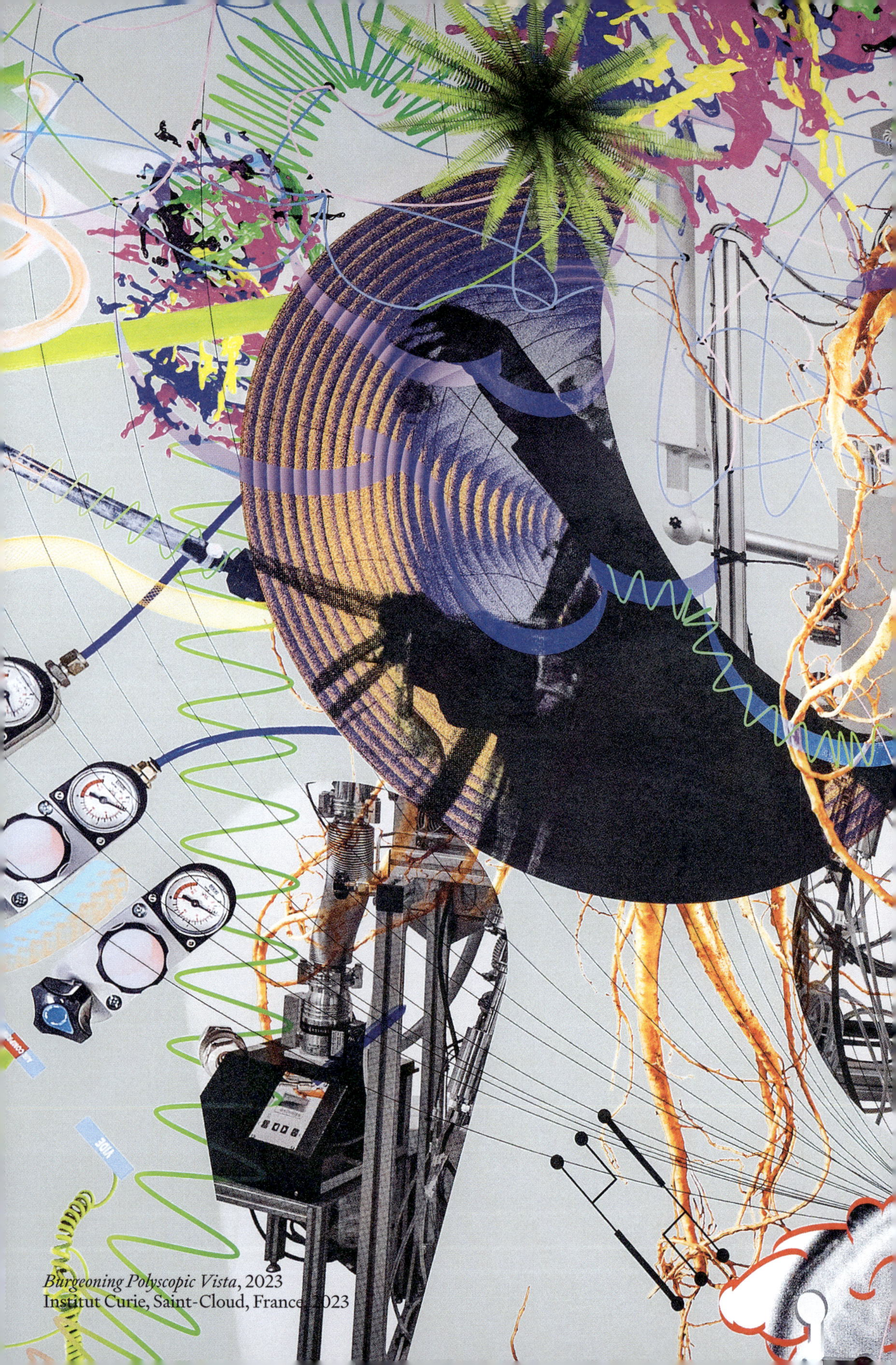

Burgeoning Polyscopic Vista, 2023
Institut Curie, Saint-Cloud, France, 2023

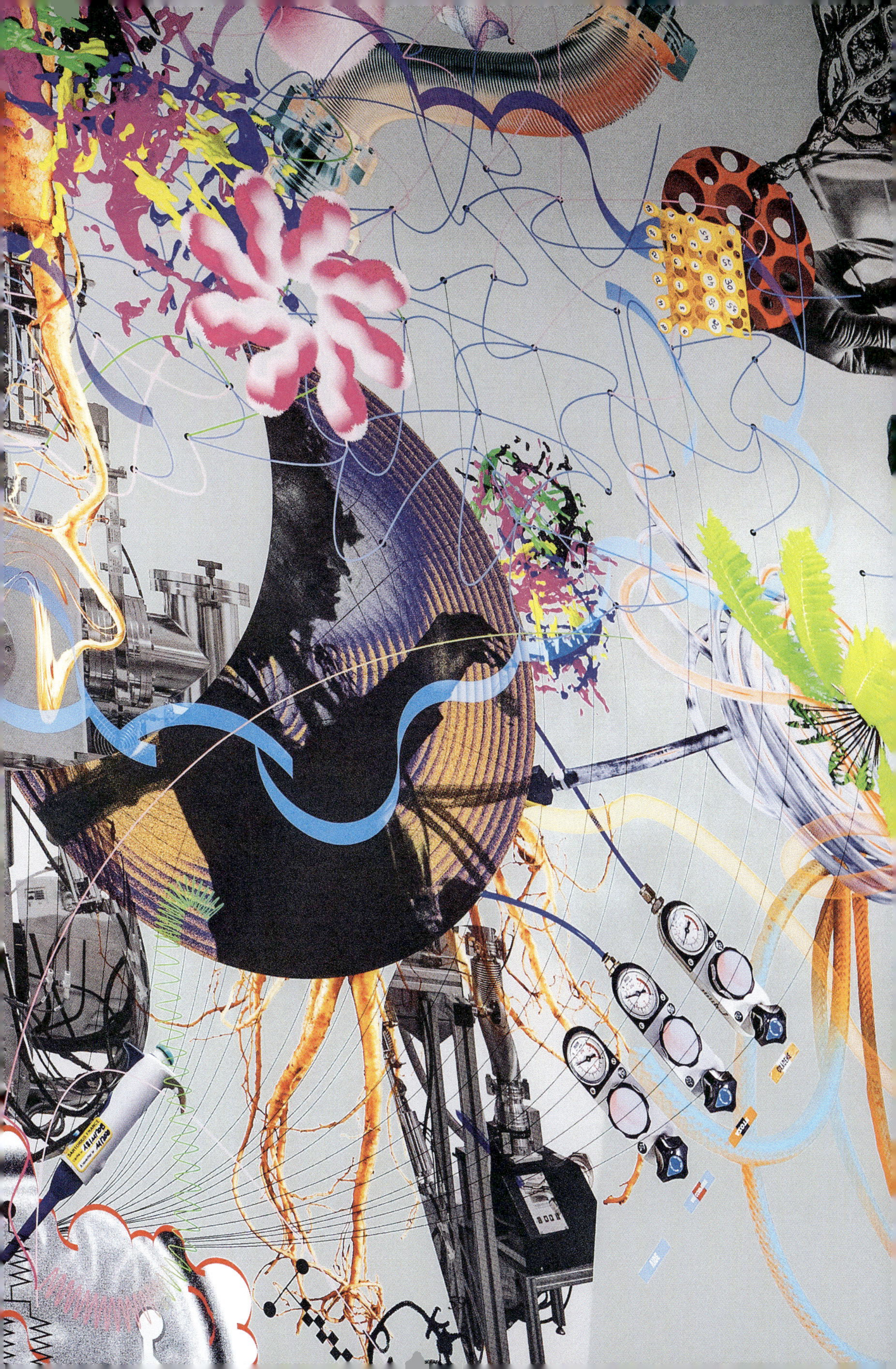

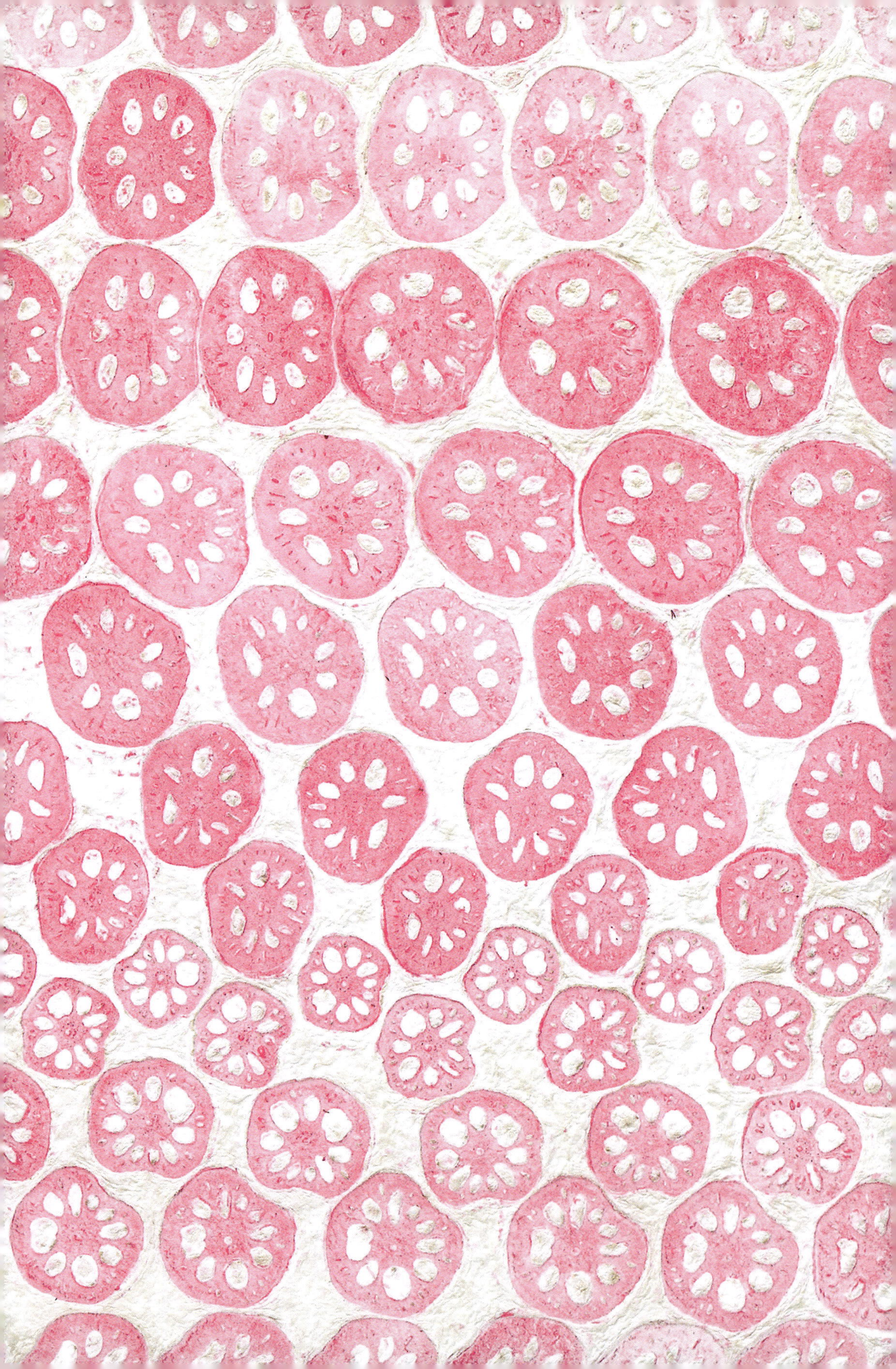

Edibles since 2012

Initiated during a residency at the Singapore Tyler Print Institute (STPI) in 2012, the *Vegetable Prints*, *Spice Sheets* and *Spice Prints* translate natural and organic ingredients from their everyday or colonial context into materials for different printing methods. This conversion from kitchen staple to artistic medium points to Yang's adherence to poor materiality and curious exploration of novel modes of production. First, for the *Spice Prints*, Yang developed a screen printing technique to adhere different spices and provisions on paper. In *Triptych Moon – Coffee, Tea, and Cacao* (2012) [Plate 32], circles made from coffee, tea, and cacao on sandpaper reveal their different textures and hues of brown as if specimens, pointing to the colonial history of violence that allowed their widespread extraction and trade. The *Vegetable Prints* document common local groceries—eggplant, bitter melon, ginger, and here lotus— through a process of *décalcomanie*, that produces two embossed prints that are mirrored images. As if a low-tech CT scan, the print indexes cross-section slices of the vegetable in faintly colored outlines created from the vegetable's natural juices. Each printed sheet documents a single unit— one vegetable, one bag of produce, or one package of spices. This is often recorded in the print's title, which includes the name of the supermarket, the product, or the product line, and underscores the importance of the origin of each object. For example, in *Edibles Diptych – Meidi-Ya, Genting Garden, Salads Royale, 176 g and 169 g* (2021) [Plate 35], the lettuce was purchased from the Singaporean supermarket chain, Meidi-Ya. The *Cutting Board Prints*, like *Cutting Board Print – Yellow Ginger #1* (2012) [Plate 34], record the movement of Yang's hand cutting through vegetables and herbs, the natural dye staining the paper along the knife's edge. Closely connected to some of the *Hardware Store Collages*, the *Vegetable* and *Spice Prints* transform everyday ingredients into colors, textures, and arrangements, abstracting them from their habitual uses to create new inventories and ledgers that subtly evoke the long histories of their global circulations and appropriations and our life in these contexts.

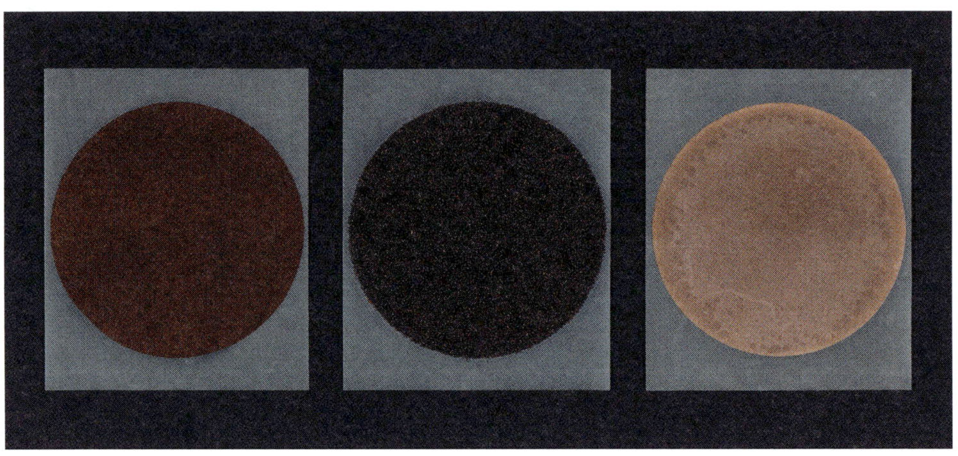

32

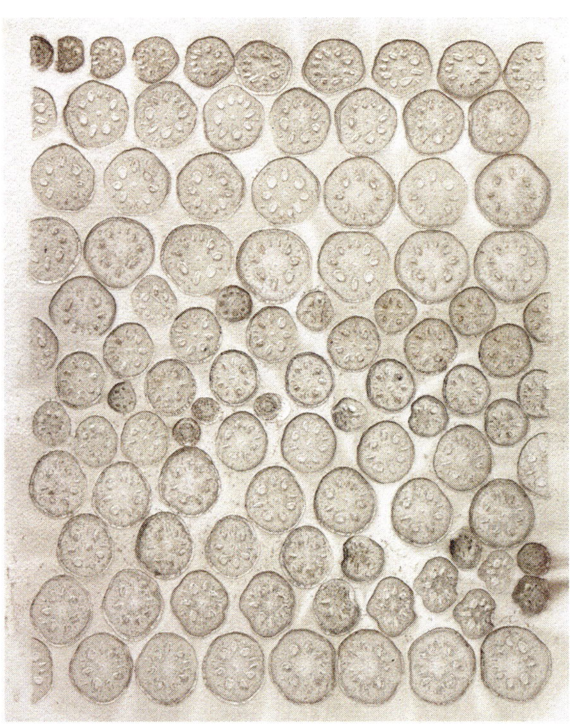

33

34

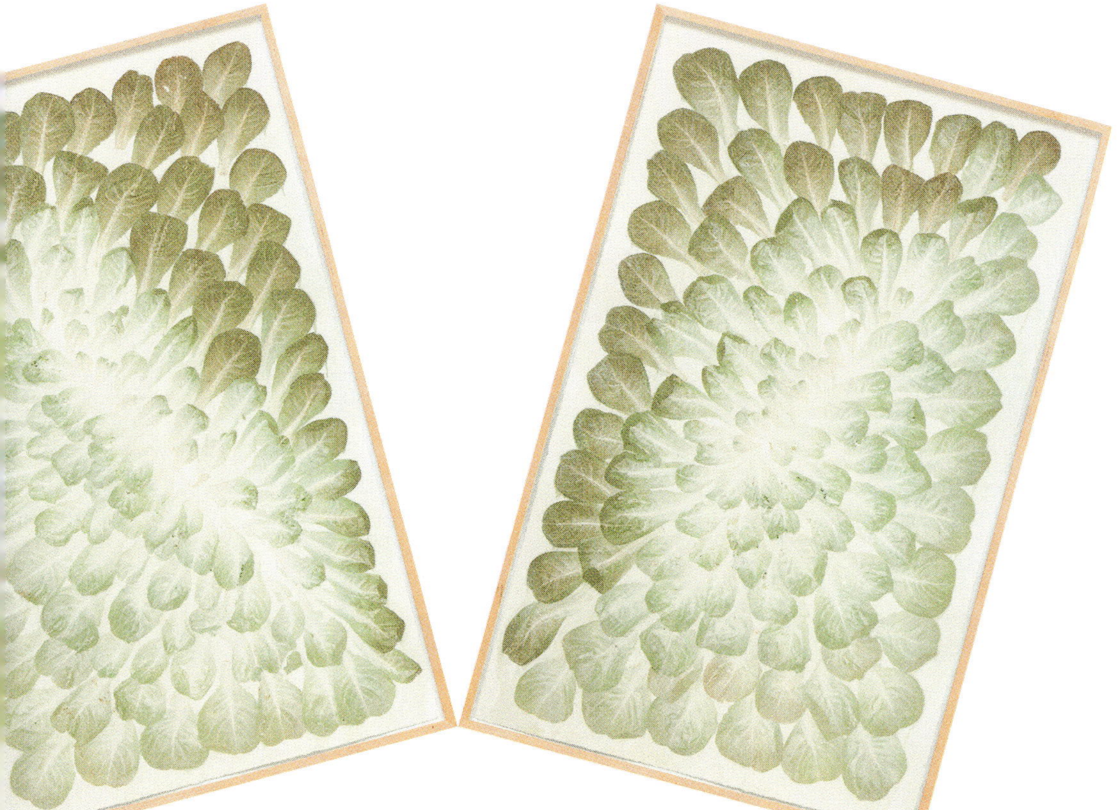

35

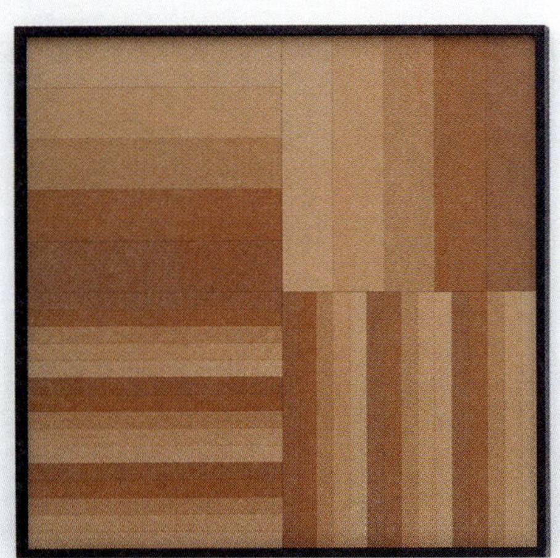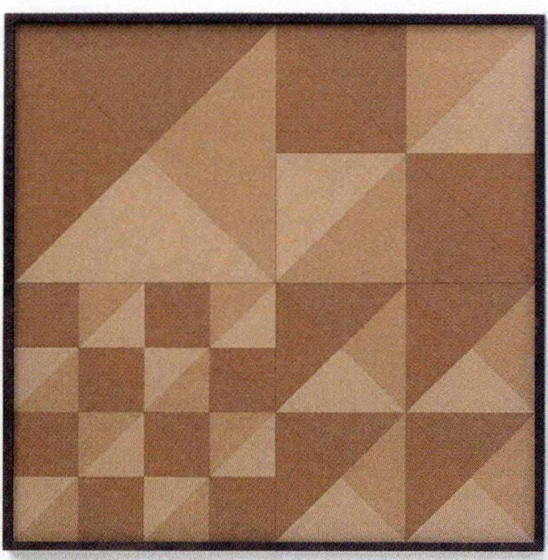

Cinnamon Sheets Composition, 2017
Monochrome Multitudes, Smart Museum of Art, The University of Chicago, United States, 2022

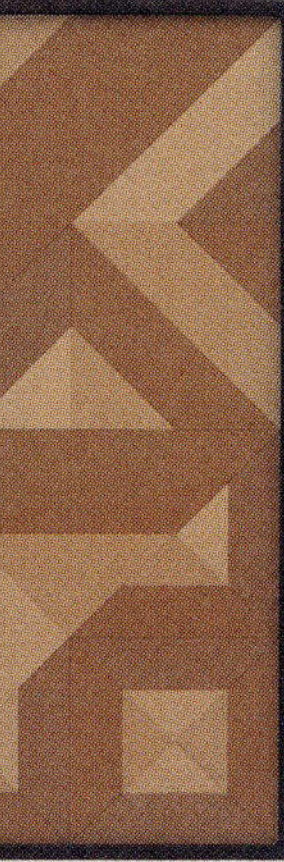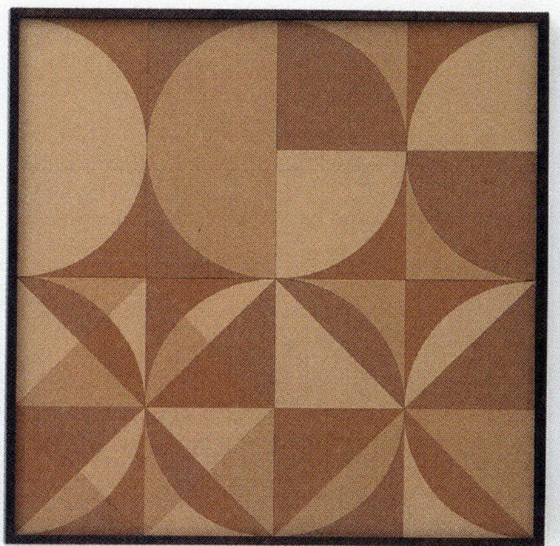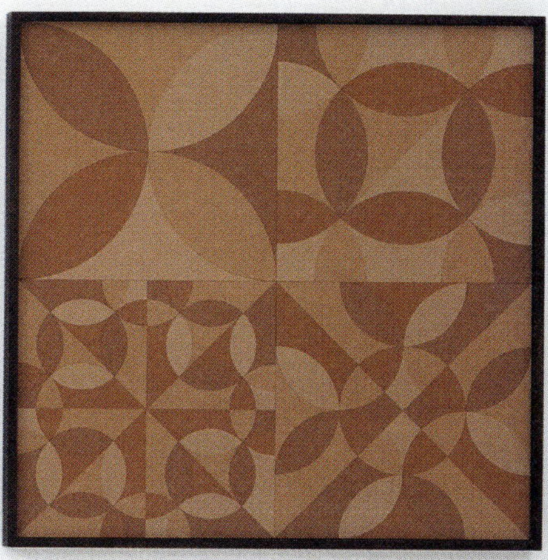

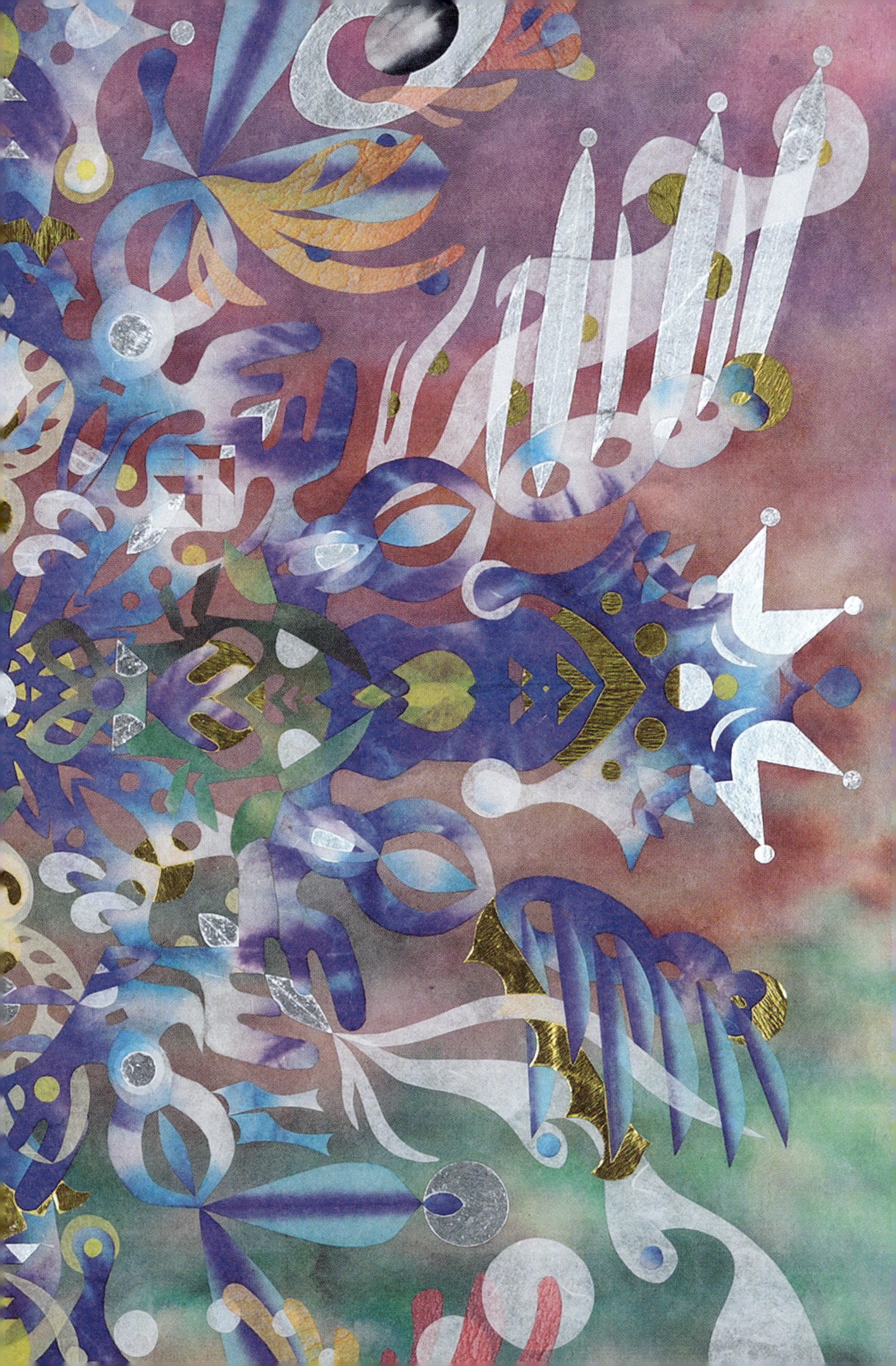

Mesmerizing Mesh since 2021

Mesmerizing Mesh is Yang's most recent series of flat works and despite having only emerged in 2021, already counts as her second most prolific flat work series after *Trustworthies*. *Mesmerizing Mesh* combine Yang's lingering research and curiosity in shamanistic and pagan rituals, folk practices, and craft works as alternative knowledge systems that have often been marginalized in society. Here Yang reorients the conceptual and material coordinates of her practice towards what she describes as "things that are minor" in a manner similar to her persistent use of poor materials in both her sculptures and flat works. Incorporating the patterns and motifs used in various papercutting traditions, especially those found in Korean shamanism and Japanese Shinto, Yang cuts and folds translucent sheets of mulberry paper, called *hanji*, into enormously intricate and abundantly ornamented collaged formations, including those kaleidoscopic, geometric, figurative, anthropomorphic or letter-incorporated. Throughout various regions, shamans mediate between different realms connecting spirits, deities, and humans during elaborate rituals using plain paper props. Additionally, the paper is animated with a soul or spirit through cuts and holes that puncture the *hanji* to allow it to breathe. Among Yang's multiple references, motifs drawn from *seolwiseolgyeong* (the tradition and technique of sacred paper cutting for rituals performed in Chungcheong Province in Korean) and *gohei* (a wooden wand decorated with zigzag paper streamers in Japan) practices form the primary visual repertoire. In *Mesmerizing Mesh*, Yang transforms the almost exclusively white palette of the ritualistic papercuts into colorful formations by using unique hand-died *hanji*. Many of the *Mesmerizing Mesh* reference specific shapes and folds used in shaman rituals—like "Sacred Conical Headgear," the paper hats shamans fold to wear for the ritual alluded to in *Shamanic Conical Headgear – Mesmerizing Mesh #1* (2021) [Plate 36]. The series can be roughly divided into two formal categories. The first contains abstract and geometric motifs based on the compositional principle of "formation" or "Sacred Wire Mesh," traditionally used to drive out evil spirits.

The other group features figurative and anthropomorphic motifs drawn from *nukjeon* (soul sheet), symbolizing the soul of the deceased in Korean shamanistic rituals.

Yang's research into the global use of paper in ritualistic and folk traditions is ever expanding to make its motifs hybrid and its composition freehand. The most recent *Mesmerizing Mesh* artworks contain and combine the floral, vegetal, and animal patterns from Slavic *wycinanki* [Plate 44], the motifs from Mexican *papel picado* or of *Catrina* [Plate 49], as well as the figurations of diverse deities of crops from the tradition of Otomí people, called *amate* [Plate 50]. The newly conceived six part installation, *Enveloped Domestic Soul Channels – Mesmerizing Mesh #208* [Pages 86–87] departs from the paper altars of the Hmong, an indigenous group residing in the border area of China, Vietnam, Myanmar, and Thailand as well as having a large diaspora in the United States. Alluding to their domestic paper altars with shamanistic tools, Yang often enshrines her collages with simple, but obviously designed, wooden structures adorned with *hanji* tassels [Pages 88–89]. Asserting the sculpture-ness of these flat objects—like traditional screens used as room dividers—Yang shifts the papercuts from the plane of the wall into the space of the gallery, a spatial leap from flat surface to interior surround.

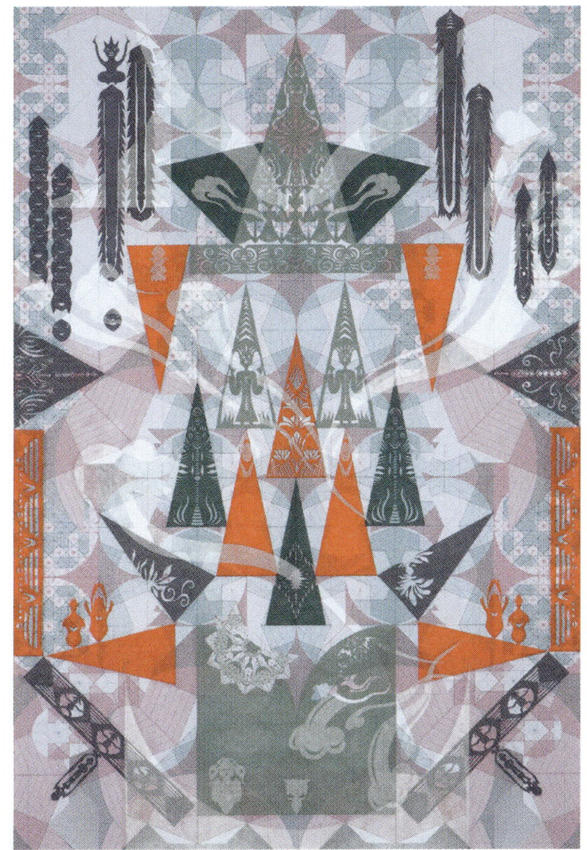

36

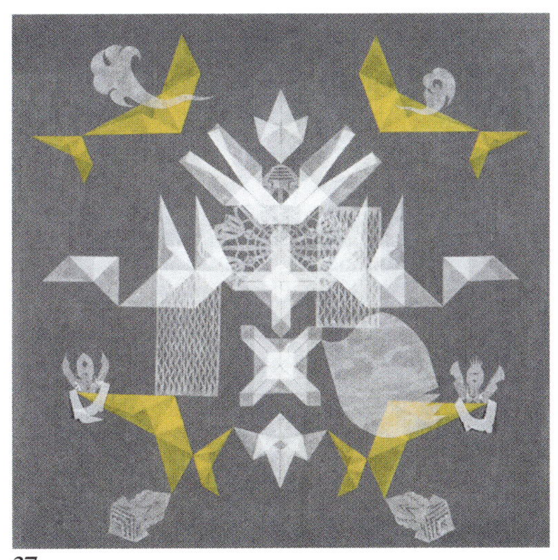

37

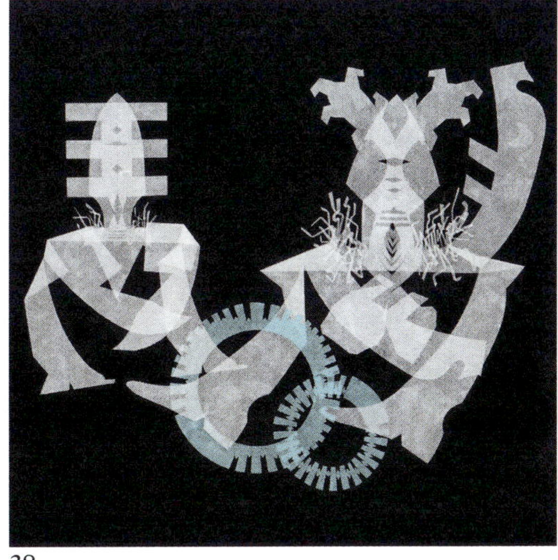

38

36 *Shamanic Conical Headgear –*
    Mesmerizing Mesh #1, 2021

37 *Ribbed Net Battle Formation –*
    Mesmerizing Mesh #8, 2021

38 *Horned Hoop-Powered*
    Soul Sheets Abreast –
    Mesmerizing Mesh #15, 2021

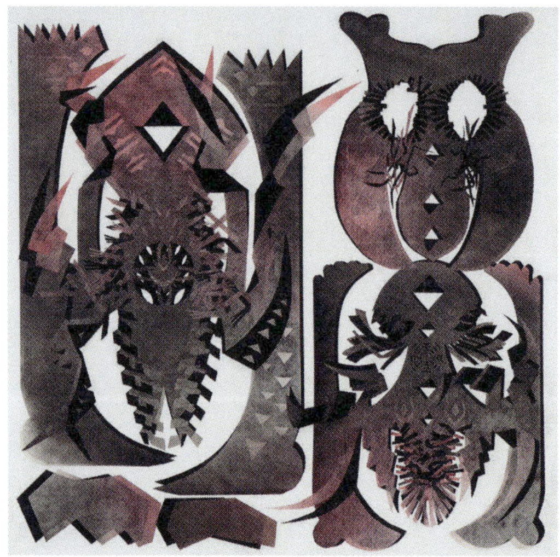

39

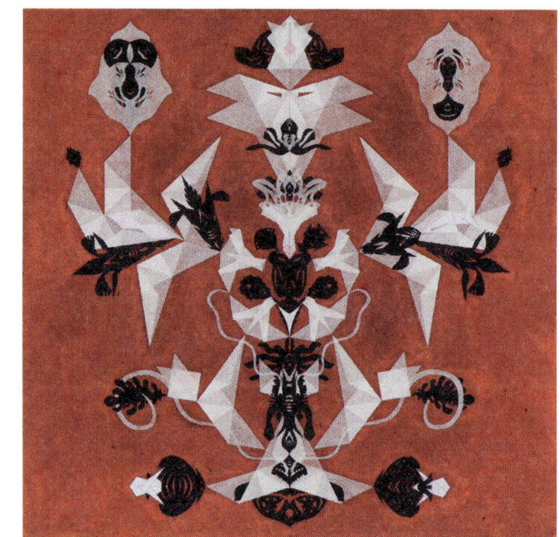

40

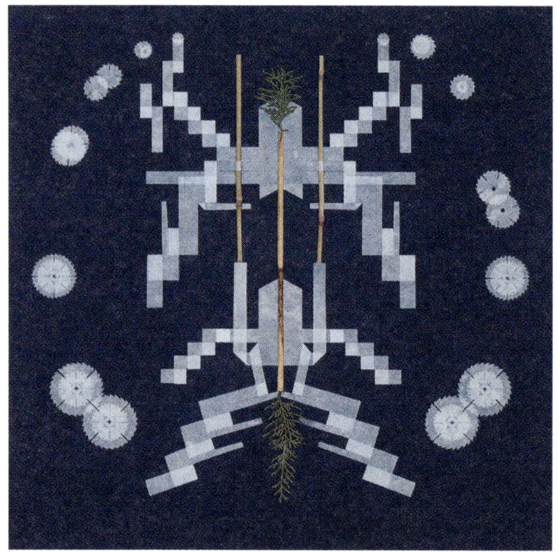

41

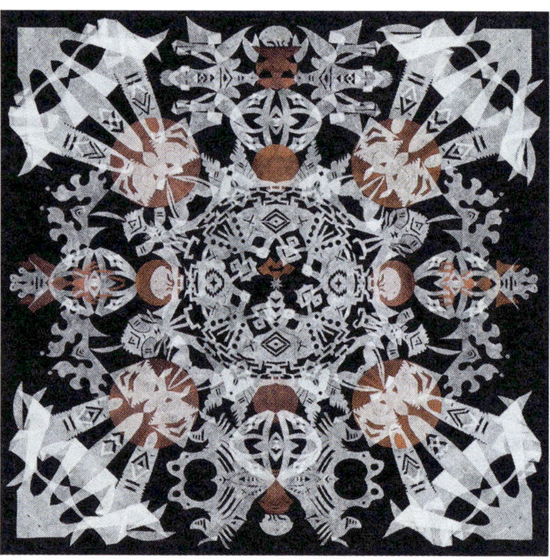

42

39 *Four-Limb-Powered Soul Sheet – Mesmerizing Mesh #24*, 2021

40 *Head Altar Formation – Mesmerizing Mesh #49*, 2021

41 *Juggling Shoulder-Lifting Soul Streamers – Mesmerizing Mesh #77*, 2021

42 *Blood Moon Finger-Pulling Bloom Formation – Mesmerizing Mesh #107*, 2022

43 *Flower Explosion Radial Folds – Mesmerizing Mesh #124*, 2022

44 *Fluoroscopic-Powered Fire Bird – Mesmerizing Mesh #130*, 2022

45 *Meditation-Powered Pagoda Tree Soul Sheet – Mesmerizing Mesh #131*, 2022

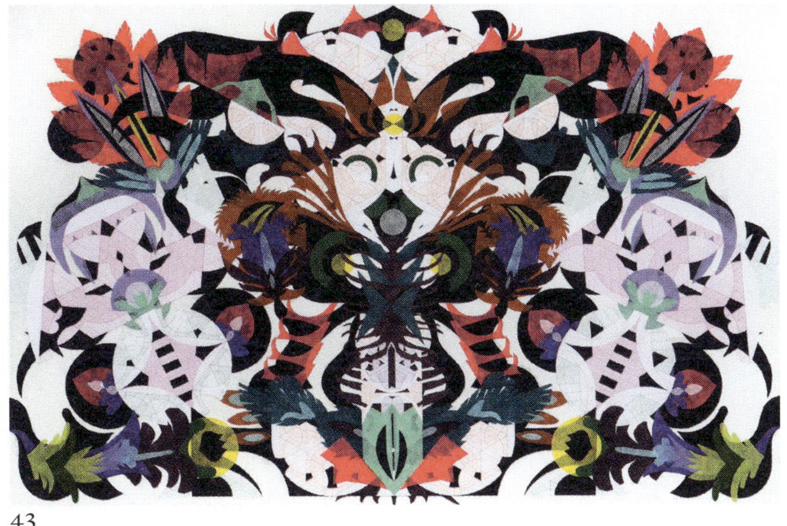

43

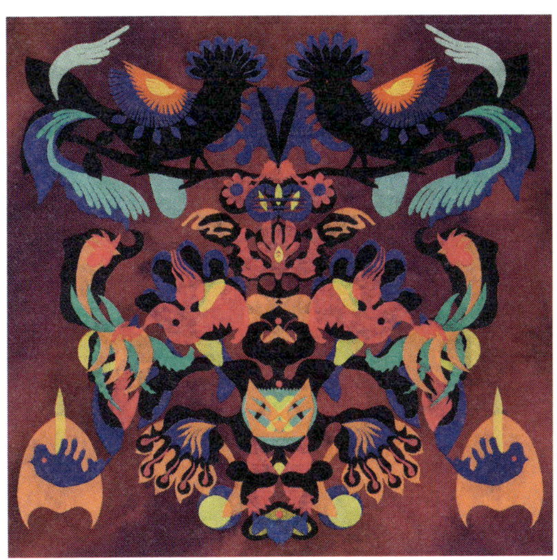

44

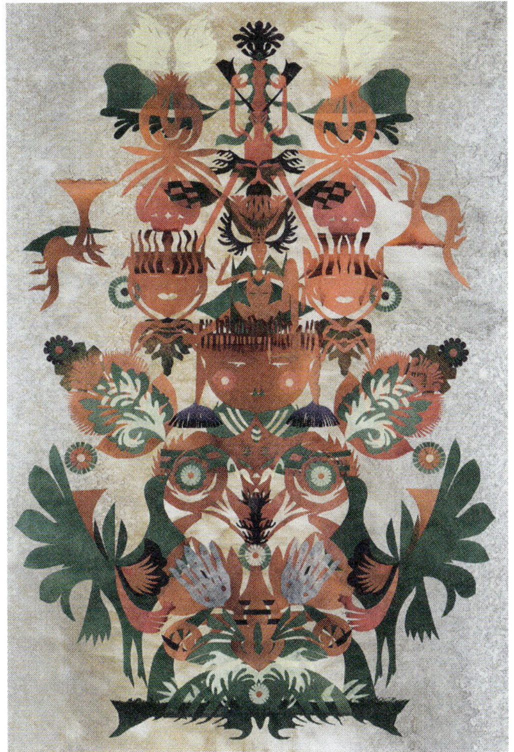

45

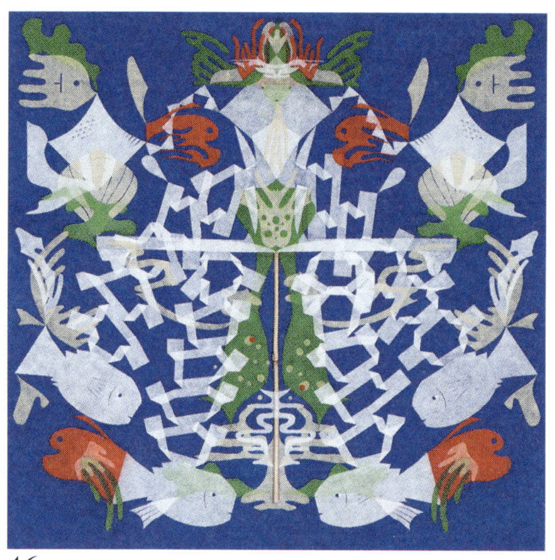

46

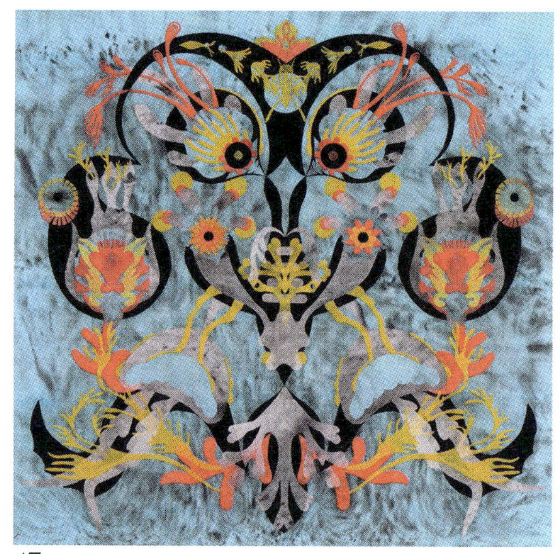

47

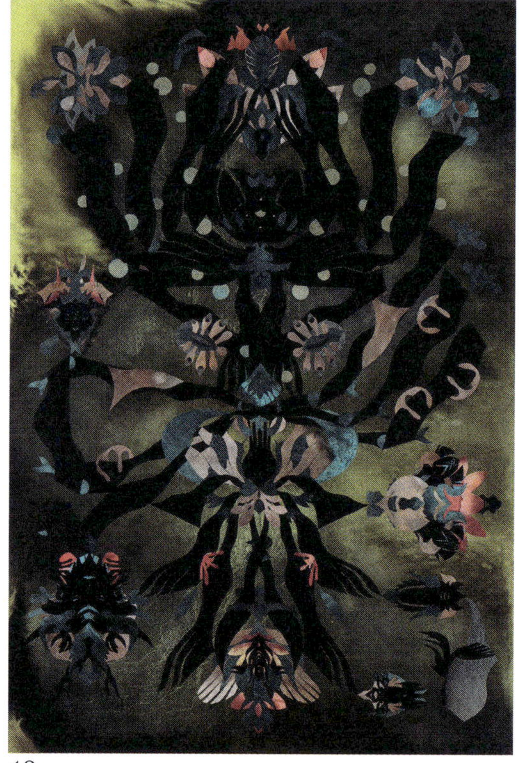

48

46 *Swaying Sea Forest Soul
Streamers – Mesmerizing
Mesh #132*, 2022

47 *Splashing Volcano Ash
Gaze – Mesmerizing
Mesh #140*, 2022

48 *Thunder-Powered Ash Entrails
Soul Streamers – Mesmerizing
Mesh #148*, 2022

49 *Day-Night Twin Catrinas
Radial Folds – Mesmerizing
Mesh #173*, 2023

50 *Rainbow Mist Germination
Soul Sheet – Mesmerizing
Mesh #184*, 2023

51 *Scattering Dawn-Light
Serenity Soul Glyph –
Mesmerizing Mesh #215*, 2023

52 *Icy Mane Woven Soul
Eyes – Mesmerizing
Mesh #236*, 2024

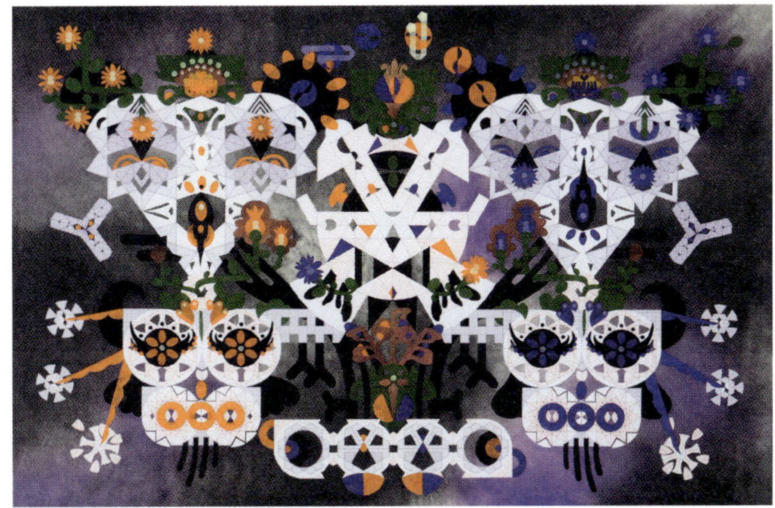

49

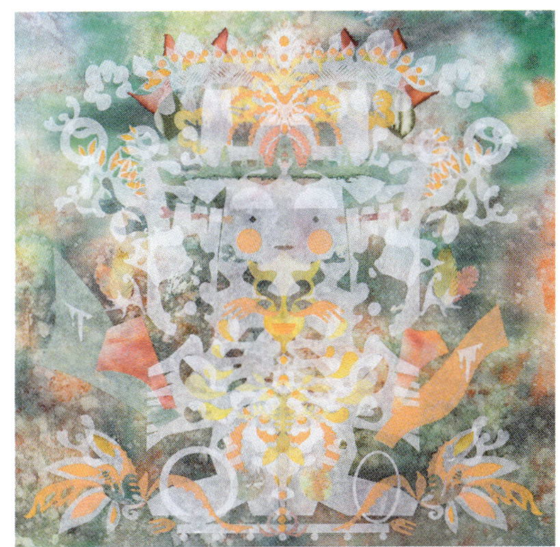

50

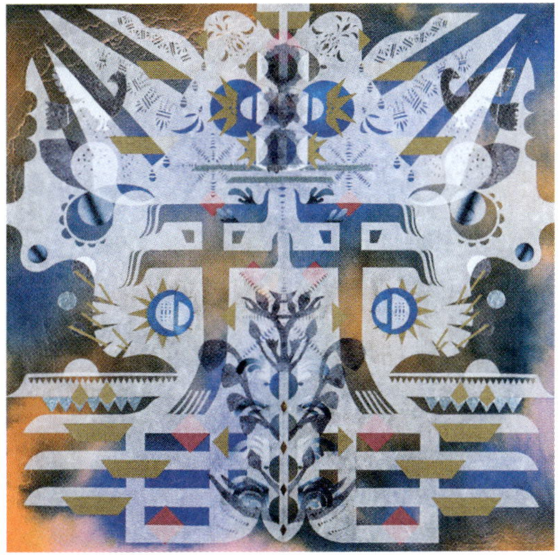

51

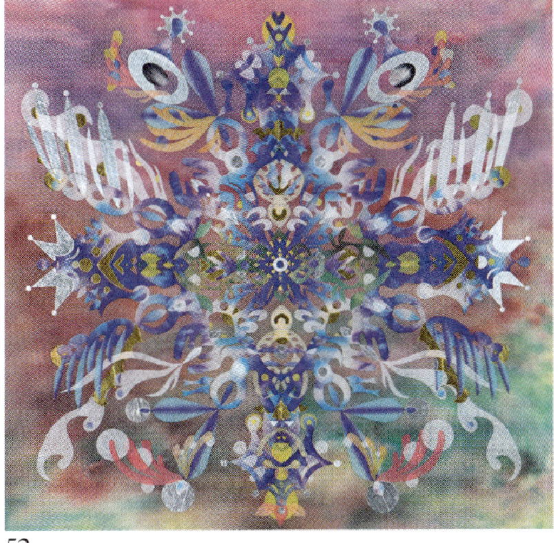

52

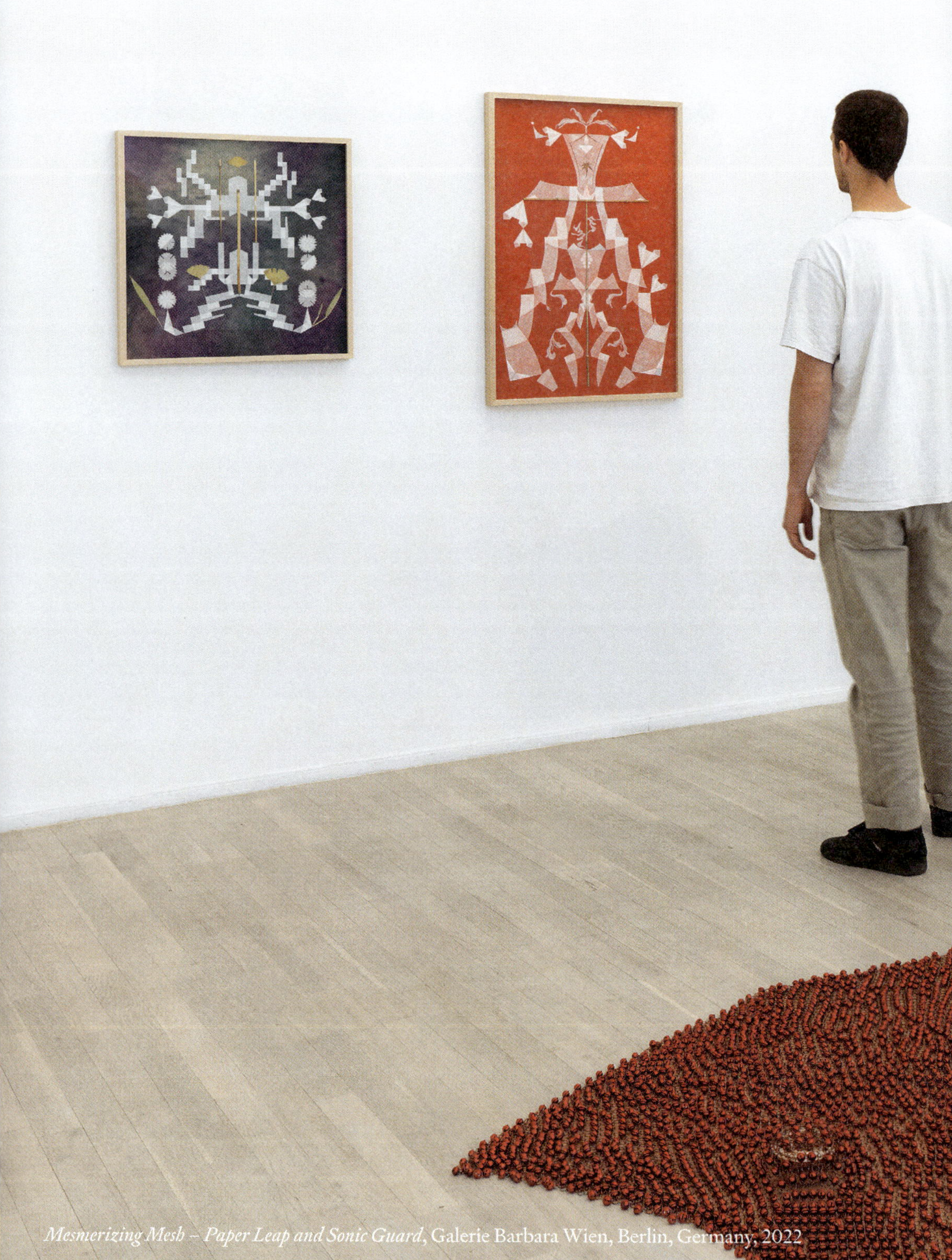

Mesmerizing Mesh – Paper Leap and Sonic Guard, Galerie Barbara Wien, Berlin, Germany, 2022

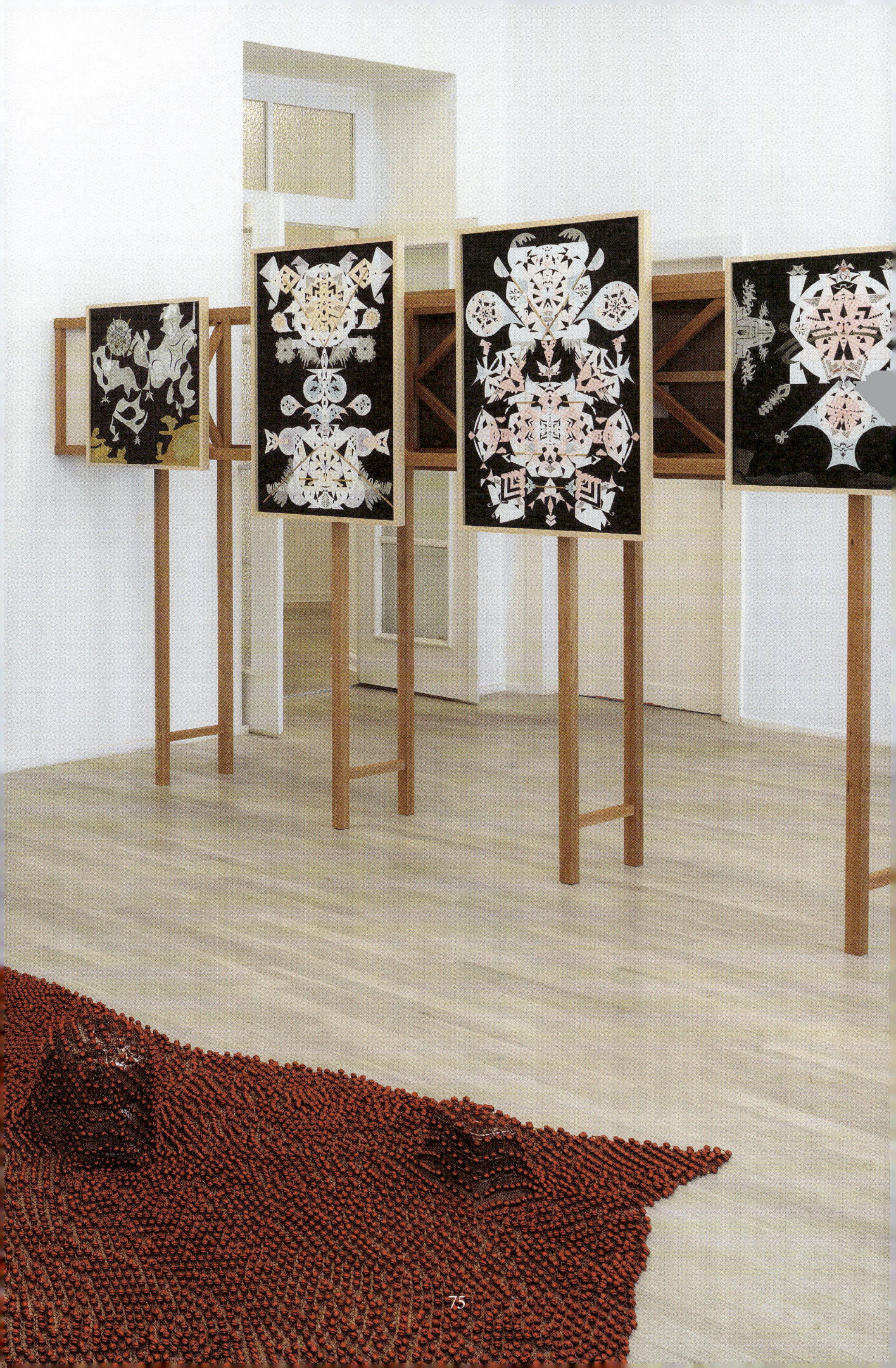

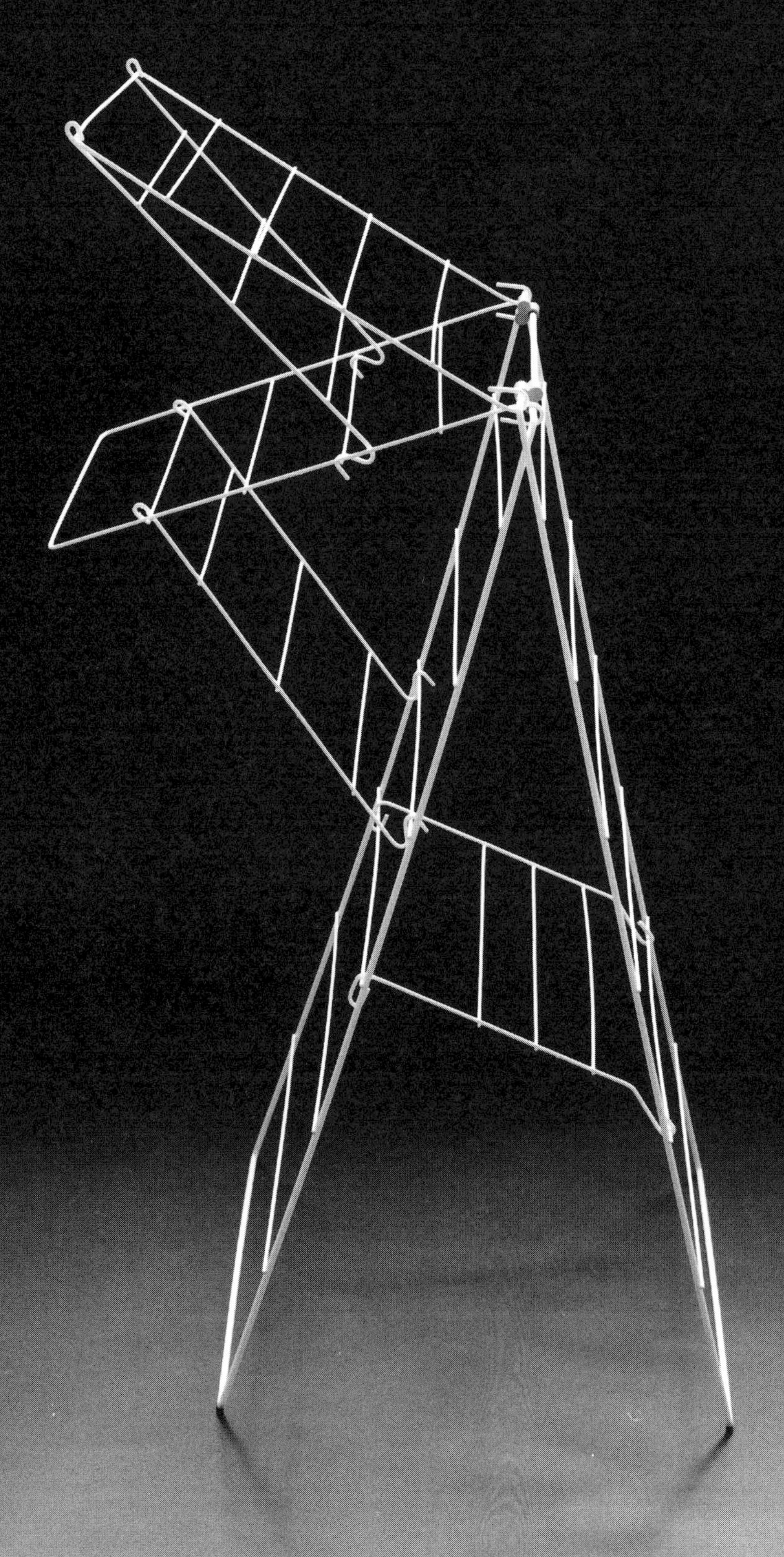

Other Flat Works

Although known for sculptures, flat works are prominent throughout Yang's oeuvre not just in series but as a range of practices from photography, drawing, print, and even publishing. Decidedly conceptual in nature, these works engage and draw out the slippages between research and documentation, knowing and unknowing, understanding and sensing.

Made in 2006, 2016, and 2023, the *Carsick Drawings* reimagine automatic drawing as an unfamiliar documentation of road trips. In the two drawings shown here [Plates 56–57], the bumps, curves, and mostly rough sections of the unpaved road between China and Vietnam are indexed by the hurried slippages of the pen from the long curling cursive-like lines that predominate along the pages. A disavowal of the standard travel log, Yang abstracts her experience as muted yet vital lines, capturing instead a trace of movement along the road and its haptic impression on her drawing hand.

Gymnastics of the Foldables (2006) [Plate 54] points to Yang's long engagement with photography, folding, and household items. The photographs document 15 different configurations of an ordinary drying rack, transforming the utilitarian object into a dancing figure. The work picks up on the shifts between two and three dimensions the drying rack undergoes—stored flat, it is animated as a sculptural object when used—paralleling the folds that transform paper into shapes in origami. Fittingly, in another photographic work, *Imperfections* (2010) [Pages 80–81], Yang documents individual origami shapes against the same gray gradient, much like the way she has the laundry rack here, creating a lexicon of motility and irregularity.

A conceptual transposition connects two different locations tethered through colonial history in *The Source of Spring is in the Trace of a Movement* (2021) [Plate 58]. Yang intentionally mis-translates an inscription written by the 19th-century British artist and social activist, Walter Crane inlaid into the floor of the South London Gallery—"The source of Art is in the Life of a People"—into Burmese. Maintaining most of the original Art Nouveau motifs of the wooden floor panel, Yang inserts the three-finger salutes adopted by pro-democracy protesters during the Spring Revolution of 2021 in Burma, and replaces the original brown tones with fresh green hues of Burmese medicinal plants. Yang's reconfiguration of Crane's socialist statement enjoins it to the contemporaneous British colonialization of Burma (1824–1948) and to the 2021 protests following a military coup, ultimately questioning which people were included in Crane's decree.

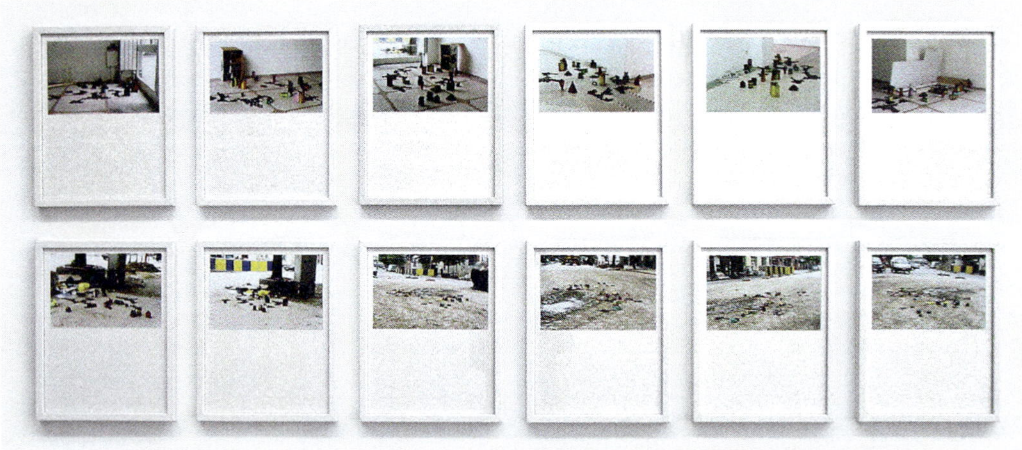

53

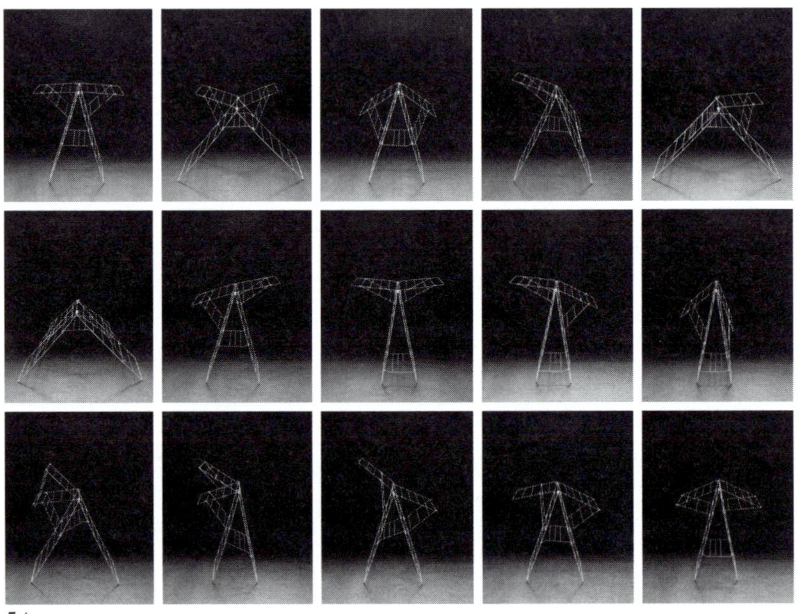

54

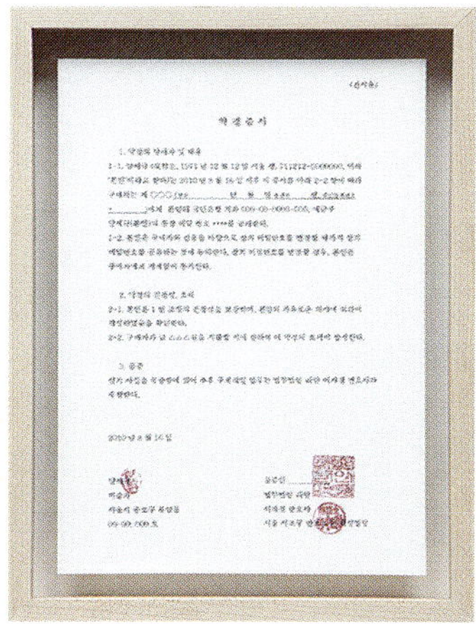

55

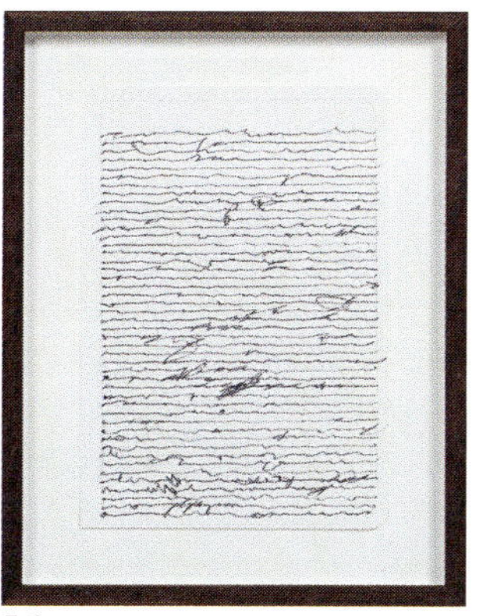

56

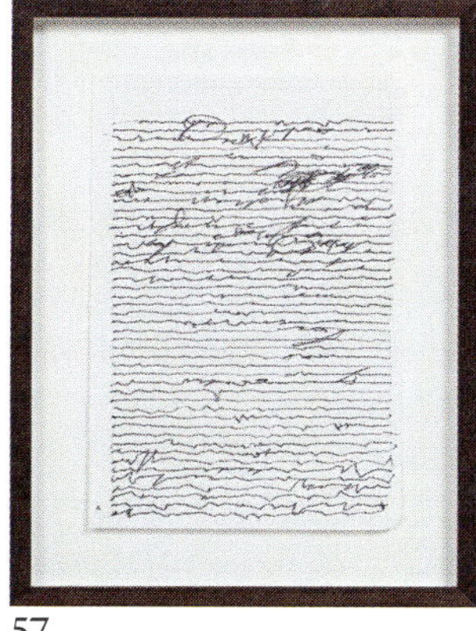

57

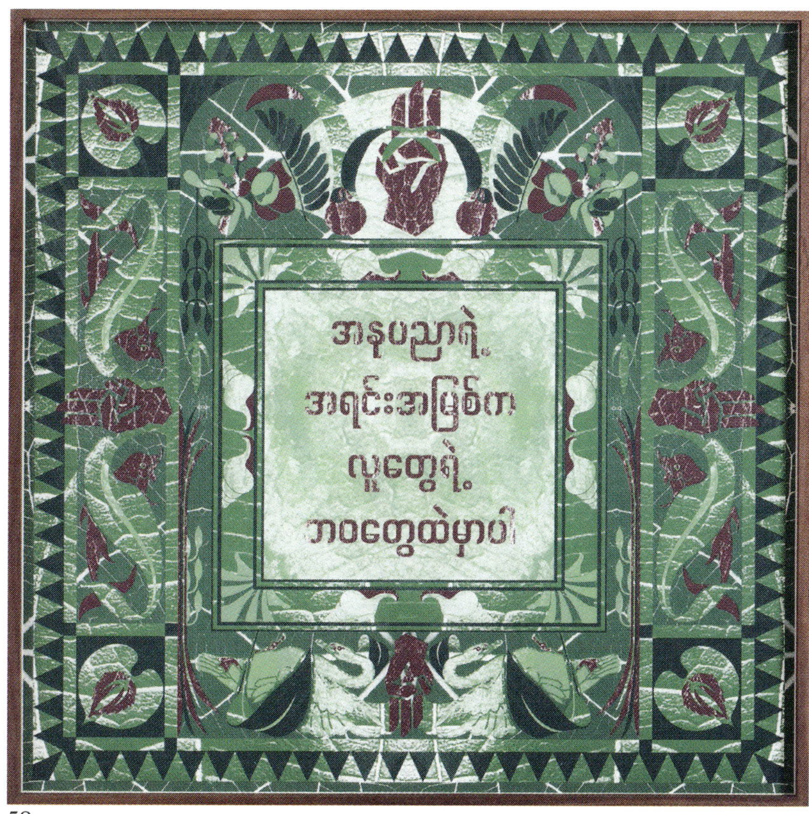

58

53 *Last Destination*
    Brussels, 2004
54 *Gymnastics of the*
    Foldables, 2006

55 *Certificate #1*, 2010
56 *Carsick Drawing –*
    Toward Huu Nghi and
    Youyiguan #1, 2016

57 *Carsick Drawing –*
    Toward Huu Nghi and
    Youyiguan #2, 2016
58 *The Source of Spring is in the*
    Trace of a Movement, 2021

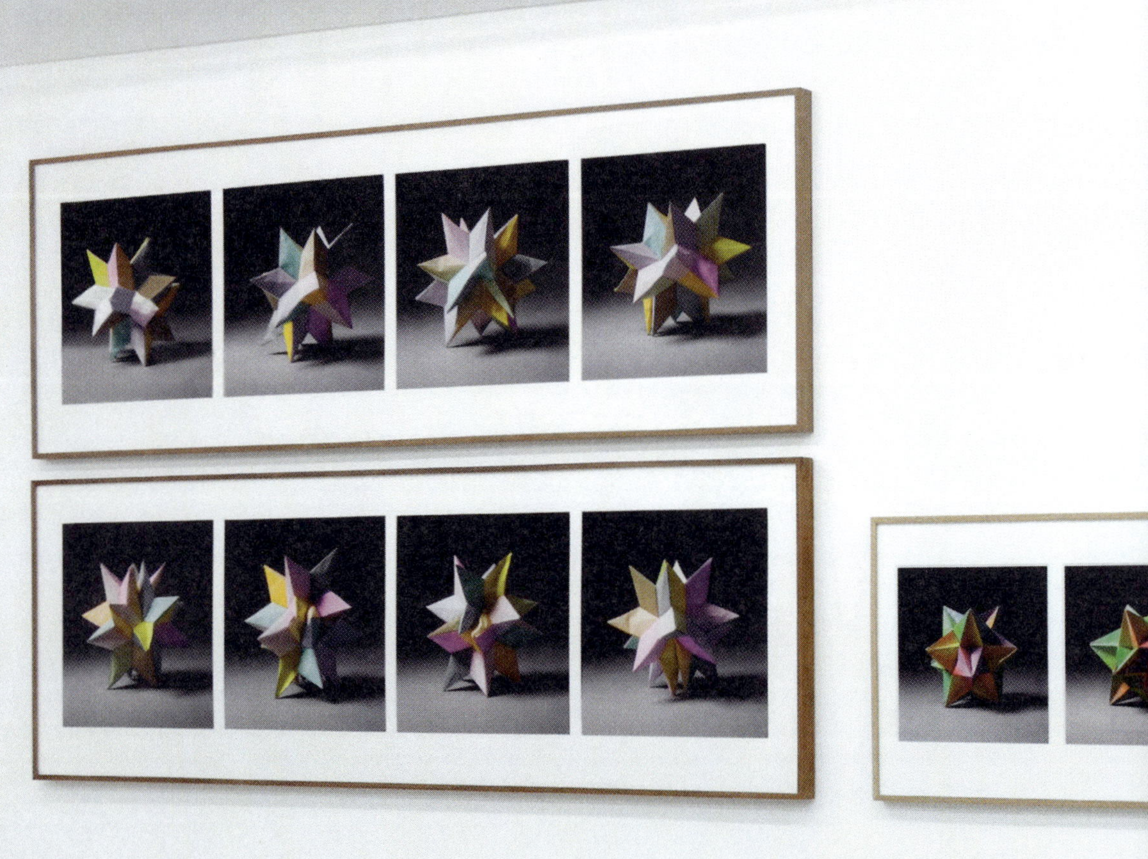

Imperfections, 2010
Family of Equivocations, Aubette 1928 and Museum of
Modern and Contemporary Art, Strasbourg, France, 2013

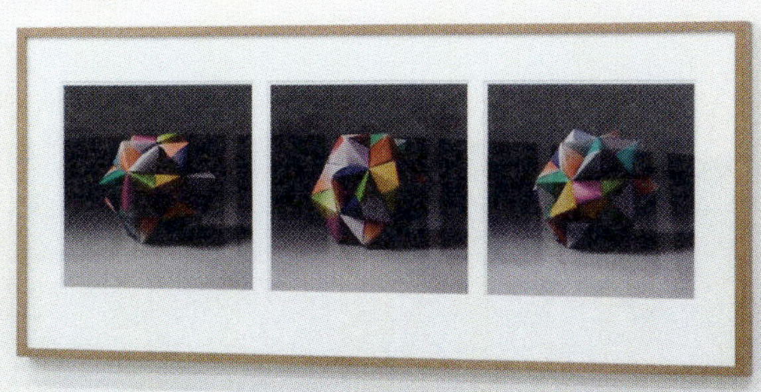

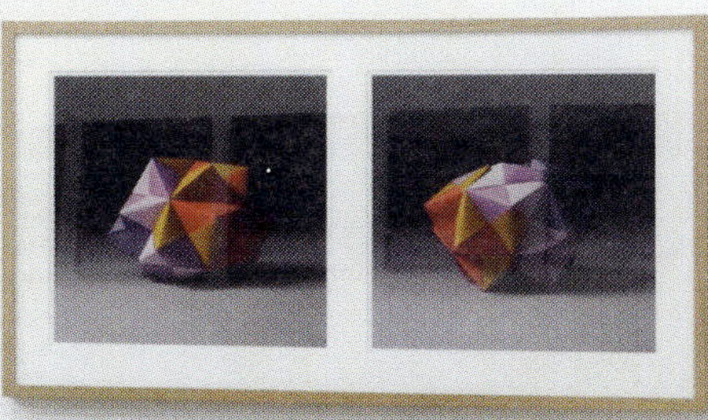

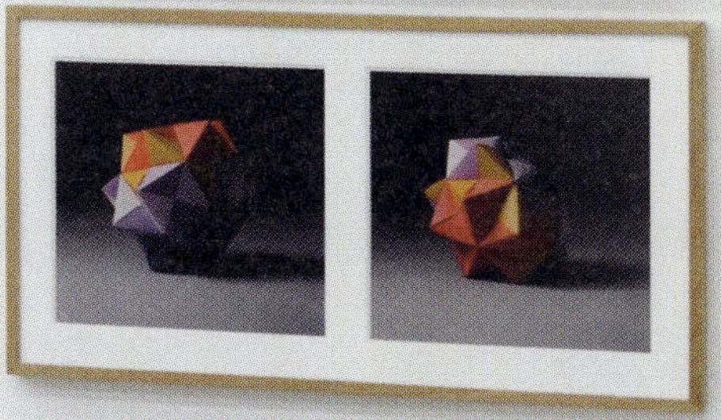

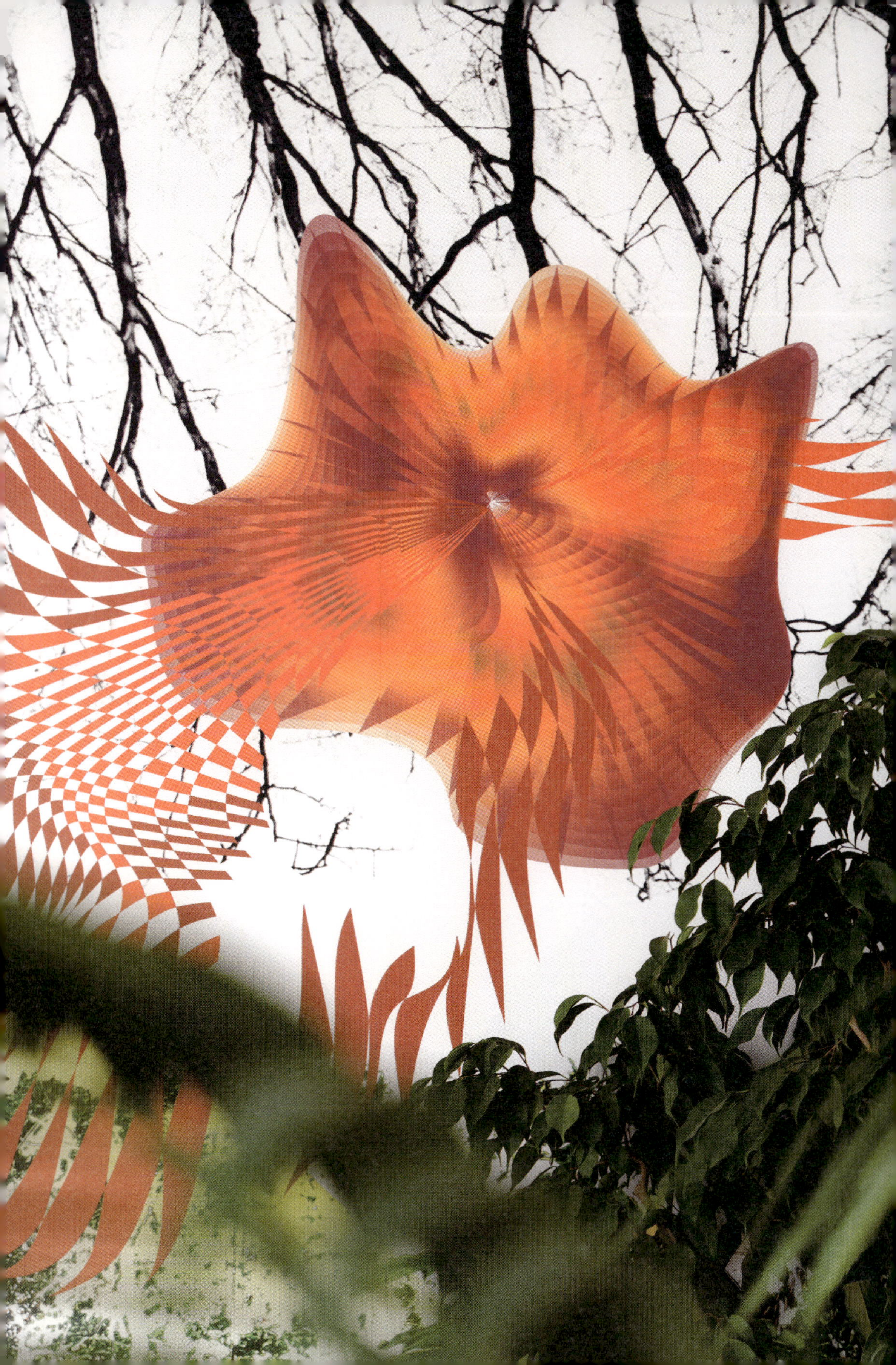

Floor Plan

54
58
36
32
44 37
46 38
47 39
50 40
Entrance
51 41
52 42
31
49 45 48 43
27 28 29 30
56 57
25 24 23 34
53
35
33
21
22
4 7 3 5 11 1 26
2 9 6 8 13 14 10 12
15 16 17 18 19 20
55

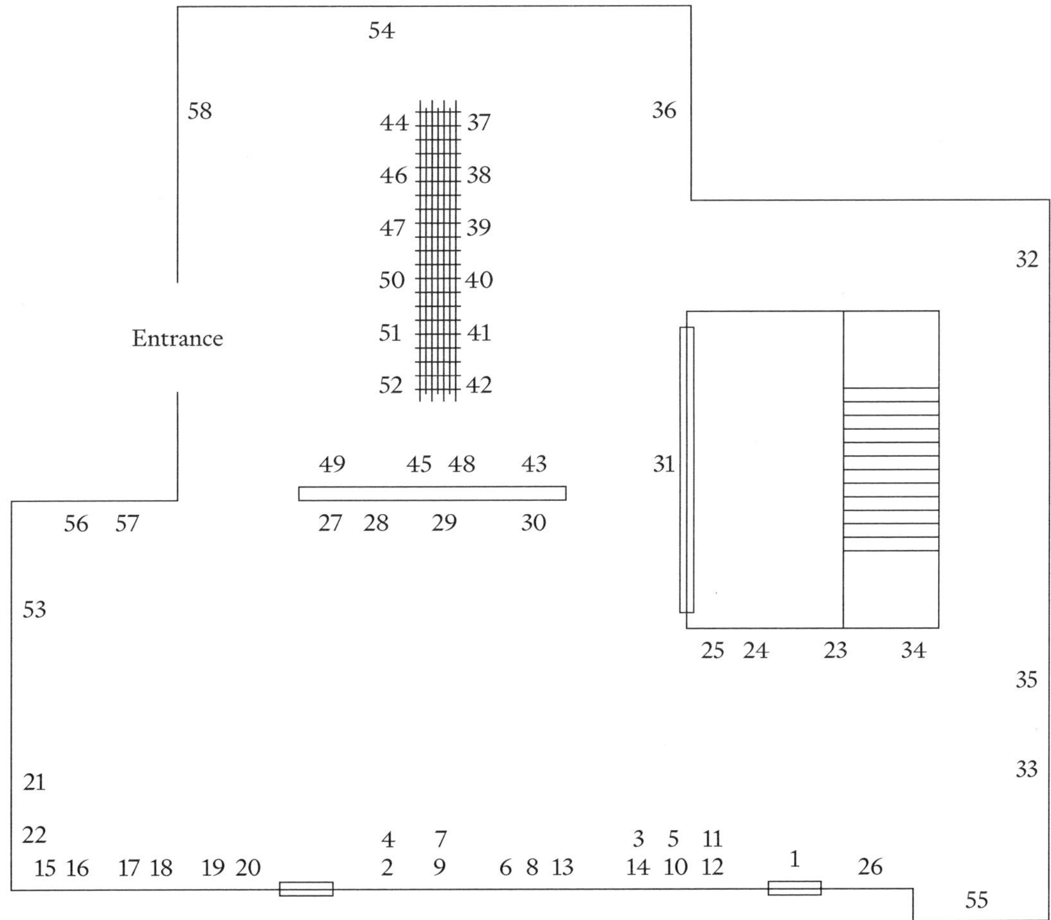

Exhibited Works

Hardware Store Collages

1 *Hornbachbuch*, 1994
Clippings from hardware
store brochures, collage
in catalogue (Stanley
Brouwn, 1 m × 1 m, ed.
Portikus, Frankfurt am
Main; Witte de With,
Rotterdam, 1993), 208 pp.

2 *Hardware Store Collage –
Bauhaus Fire Places #1*, 2013
Clippings from hardware
store catalogues on
French marbled paper,
mounted on alu-dibond
51.2 × 66.2 cm[+]

3 *Hardware Store Collage –
Bauhaus Kitchen Sinks #1*, 2013
Clippings from hardware
store catalogues on
chromolux paper,
mounted on alu-dibond
51.2 × 36.2 cm[+]

4 *Hardware Store Collage –
Bauhaus Mirrors #1*, 2013
Clippings from hardware
store catalogues on
French marbled paper,
mounted on alu-dibond
51.2 × 66.2 cm[+]

5 *Hardware Store Collage –
Schäfer Furniture
Dollies #1*, 2014
Clippings from mail-
order catalogues on
chromolux paper,
mounted on alu-dibond
51.2 × 36.2 cm[+]

6 *Hardware Store Collage –
Schäfer Ballpoints and
Mechanical Pencils #1*, 2015
Clippings from mail-order
catalogues on chromolux
paper, mounted on
alu-dibond, frame
71.2 × 51.2 cm

7 *Hardware Store Collage –
Schäfer Wall Clocks #1*, 2015
Clippings from mail-
order catalogues on
chromolux paper,
mounted on alu-dibond
51.2 × 71.2 cm[+]

8 *Hardware Store Collage –
Schäfer Protection
Barriers #1*, 2015
Clippings from mail-
order catalogues on
chromolux paper,
mounted on alu-dibond
71.2 × 51.2 cm[+]

9 *Hardware Store Collage –
Schäfer Office Chairs #1*, 2015
Clippings from mail-
order catalogues on
chromolux paper,
mounted on alu-dibond
51.2 × 71.2 cm[+]

10 *Hardware Store Collage –
Bauhaus Outdoor
Lamps #1*, 2017
Clippings from hardware
store catalogues on
chromolux paper,
mounted on alu-dibond
51.2 × 36.2 cm[+]

11 *Hardware Store Collage –
Schäfer Trash Cans and
Ashtrays #1*, 2017
Clippings from mail-
order catalogues on
chromolux paper,
mounted on alu-dibond
51.2 × 36.2 cm[+]

12 *Hardware Store Collage –
OBI Mailboxes #1*, 2017
Clippings from mail-order
catalogues on chromolux
paper, mounted on
alu-dibond, frame
51.2 × 36.2 cm

13 *Hardware Store Collage –
Schäfer Storage Boxes #1*, 2017
Clippings from mail-
order catalogues on
chromolux paper,
mounted on alu-dibond
71.2 × 51.2 cm[+]

14 *Hardware Store Collage –
Leica Microsystems Clinic and
Surgery Microscopes #1*, 2019
Clippings from medical
device brochures on
chromolux paper,
mounted on alu-dibond
51.2 × 36.2 cm[+]

Lacquer Paintings

15 *Yew Dust of Villeperdue
Dripping Over*, 2016
Chipboard, wood
varnish, dust
75 × 55 cm

16 *Midsummer Dust, Dirt,
and Grit in the Breeze of
Saché*, 2015–2017
Chipboard, wood varnish,
seedpod, insects
77 × 55 cm

17 *Bunched and Bent –
Onions, 250 g*, 2018
Chipboard, wood varnish,
graph paper, mesh
produce bag, dust
25 × 17.5 × 2.6 cm

18 *Teeth Schema Shaken*, 2019
Chipboard, wood varnish,
seeds, electrical wire
crimps, dust, insects, hair
20 × 20 × 2.4 cm

19 *Unknown Schema*, 2019
Chipboard, wood varnish,
seeds, clock hands, electrical
wire crimps, dust, insect, hair
35 × 56.5 × 2.3 cm

20 *Pollen Sneeze*, 2019
Chipboard, wood varnish,
seeds, found plants, mesh
produce bag parts, pins,
dust, insects, hair
45 × 45 × 3 cm

21 *A Frizzled Look*, 2023
Chipboard, wood varnish,
seeds, wig, dust, insects, hair
35 × 25 × 2 cm

22 *Hairy Shatters*, 2023
Chipboard, wood varnish,
wig, chains, dust, insect, hair
35 × 25 × 2 cm

Non-Foldings

23 *Non-Folding – Geometric
Tipping #15*, 2013
Spray paint on paper
142.6 × 102.6 cm[+]

24 *Non-Folding – Geometric
Tipping #59*, 2015
Spray paint on paper
100 × 72 cm[+]

25 *Non-Folding – Geometric
Tipping #65*, 2015
Spray paint on paper
100 × 72 cm[+]

26 *Non-Folding – Scenarios
of Non-Geometric
Folding #15*, 2015
Flattened origami objects,
spray paint, and graph
paper on cardboard
72.2 × 72.2 cm[+]

Trustworthies

27 *Trustworthy Wave #24*, 2010
Various security
envelopes and graph
paper on cardboard
102.2 × 72.2 cm[+]

28 *Trustworthy Turban*

#165, 2012
Various security
envelopes and graph
paper on cardboard
102.2 × 72.2 cm[+]

29 *Nonprofit – Trustworthy
#179*, 2012
Various security
envelopes and graph
paper on cardboard
36.2 × 51.2 cm[+]

30 *Scanning Hot Inner Values –
Trustworthy #378*, 2019
Various security envelopes,
graph paper, laser prints,
self-adhesive holographic
and reflective vinyl
film on alu-dibond
2 parts, 57.2 × 57.2 cm each[+]

Wallpapers

31 *Incantations –
Entwinement, Endurance,
and Extinction*, 2022
Digital color print on
self-adhesive vinyl film[**]
Dimensions variable

Edibles[***]

32 *Triptych Moon – Coffee,
Tea, and Cacao*, 2012
Screen prints, sandpaper,
coffee, tea, cacao
41 × 88 cm[+]
Courtesy of Kukje Gallery

33 *Vegetable Print – Lotus
Natural #2*, 2012
Embossing, natural
dye, STPI handmade
paper, lotus root
80.5 × 64.5 cm[+]

34 *Cutting Board Print –
Yellow Ginger #1*, 2012
Natural dye, 100% cotton
paper, turmeric
26.5 × 33.5 cm[+]

35 *Edibles Diptych – Meidi-Ya,
Genting Garden, Salads
Royale, 176 g and 169 g*, 2021
Vegetable pressed on paper
2 parts, 91.5 × 57.5 cm each[+]

Mesmerizing Mesh

36 *Shamanic Conical Headgear –
Mesmerizing Mesh #1*, 2021
Hanji, graph paper
on alu-dibond
122 × 82 cm[+]

37 *Ribbed Net Battle Formation –
Mesmerizing Mesh #8*, 2021

Hanji on alu-dibond
62 × 62 cm[+]

38 *Horned Hoop-Powered Soul
Sheets Abreast – Mesmerizing
Mesh #15*, 2021
Hanji on alu-dibond
62 × 62 cm[+]

39 *Four-Limb-Powered Soul
Sheet – Mesmerizing
Mesh #24*, 2021
Hanji on alu-dibond
62 × 62 cm[+]

40 *Head Altar Formation –
Mesmerizing Mesh #49*, 2021
Hanji, graph paper
on alu-dibond
62 × 62 cm[+]

41 *Juggling Shoulder-Lifting
Soul Streamers – Mesmerizing
Mesh #77*, 2021
Hanji, leaves, reed
sticks on alu-dibond
62 × 62 cm[+]

42 *Blood Moon Finger-
Pulling Bloom Formation –
Mesmerizing Mesh #107*, 2022
Hanji on alu-dibond
62 × 62 cm[+]

43 *Flower Explosion Radial
Folds – Mesmerizing
Mesh #124*, 2022
Hanji, graph paper
on alu-dibond
62 × 92 cm[+]

44 *Fluoroscopic-Powered
Fire Bird – Mesmerizing
Mesh #130*, 2022
Hanji on alu-dibond
62 × 62 cm[+]

45 *Meditation-Powered Pagoda
Tree Soul Sheet – Mesmerizing
Mesh #131*, 2022
Hanji on alu-dibond
92 × 62 cm[+]

46 *Swaying Sea Forest Soul
Streamers – Mesmerizing
Mesh #132*, 2022
Hanji, reed stick
on alu-dibond
62 × 62 cm[+]

47 *Splashing Volcano Ash Gaze –
Mesmerizing Mesh #140*, 2022
Hanji on alu-dibond
62 × 62 cm[+]

48 *Thunder-Powered Ash Entrails
Soul Streamers – Mesmerizing
Mesh #148*, 2022
Hanji on alu-dibond
92 × 62 cm[+]

49 *Day-Night Twin Catrinas*

*Radial Folds – Mesmerizing
Mesh #173*, 2023
Hanji, washi, graph paper on
alu-dibond
62 × 92 cm[+]

50 *Rainbow Mist Germination
Soul Sheet – Mesmerizing
Mesh #184*, 2023
Hanji, washi on alu-dibond
62 × 62 cm[+]

51 *Scattering Dawn-Light
Serenity Soul Glyph –
Mesmerizing Mesh #215*, 2023
Hanji, washi on alu-dibond
62 × 62 cm[+]

52 *Icy Mane Woven Soul Eyes –
Mesmerizing Mesh #236*,
2024[^]
Hanji, washi, origami
paper on alu-dibond
62 × 62 cm[+]
Collection The Arts
Club of Chicago

Other Flat Works

53 *Last Destination Brussels*, 2004
12 C-Prints
31.5 × 24.5 cm each[+]

54 *Gymnastics of the
Foldables*, 2006
15 b/w photographs
34.8 × 28.1 cm each[+]

55 *Certificate #1*, 2010
Laser print
35.5 × 27 cm[+]

56 *Carsick Drawing –
Toward Huu Nghi and
Youyiguan #1*, 2016
Ink on paper
28 × 21.5 cm[+]

57 *Carsick Drawing –
Toward Huu Nghi and
Youyiguan #2*, 2016
Ink on paper
28 × 21.5 cm[+]

58 *The Source of Spring is in the
Trace of a Movement*, 2021
Screenprint on paper
with debossing
62 × 62 cm[+]

[*] All works courtesy of the
artist unless otherwise noted

[**] *Incantations – Entwinement,
Endurance, and Extinction*
omits paper pinwheels
as installed in Chicago

[***] All *Edibles* produced at
STPI – Creative Workshop
& Gallery, Singapore

[+] Framed size

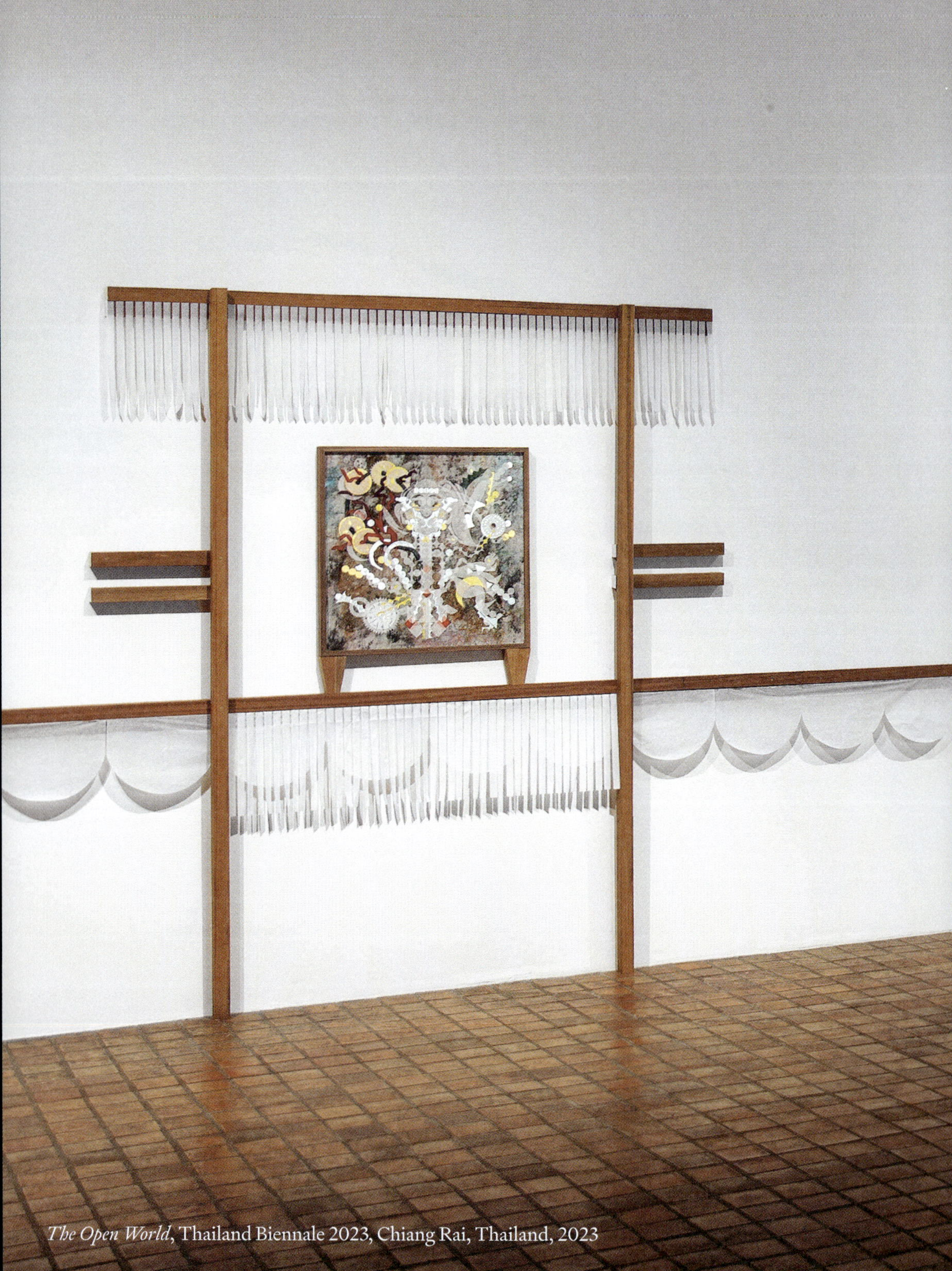

The Open World, Thailand Biennale 2023, Chiang Rai, Thailand, 2023

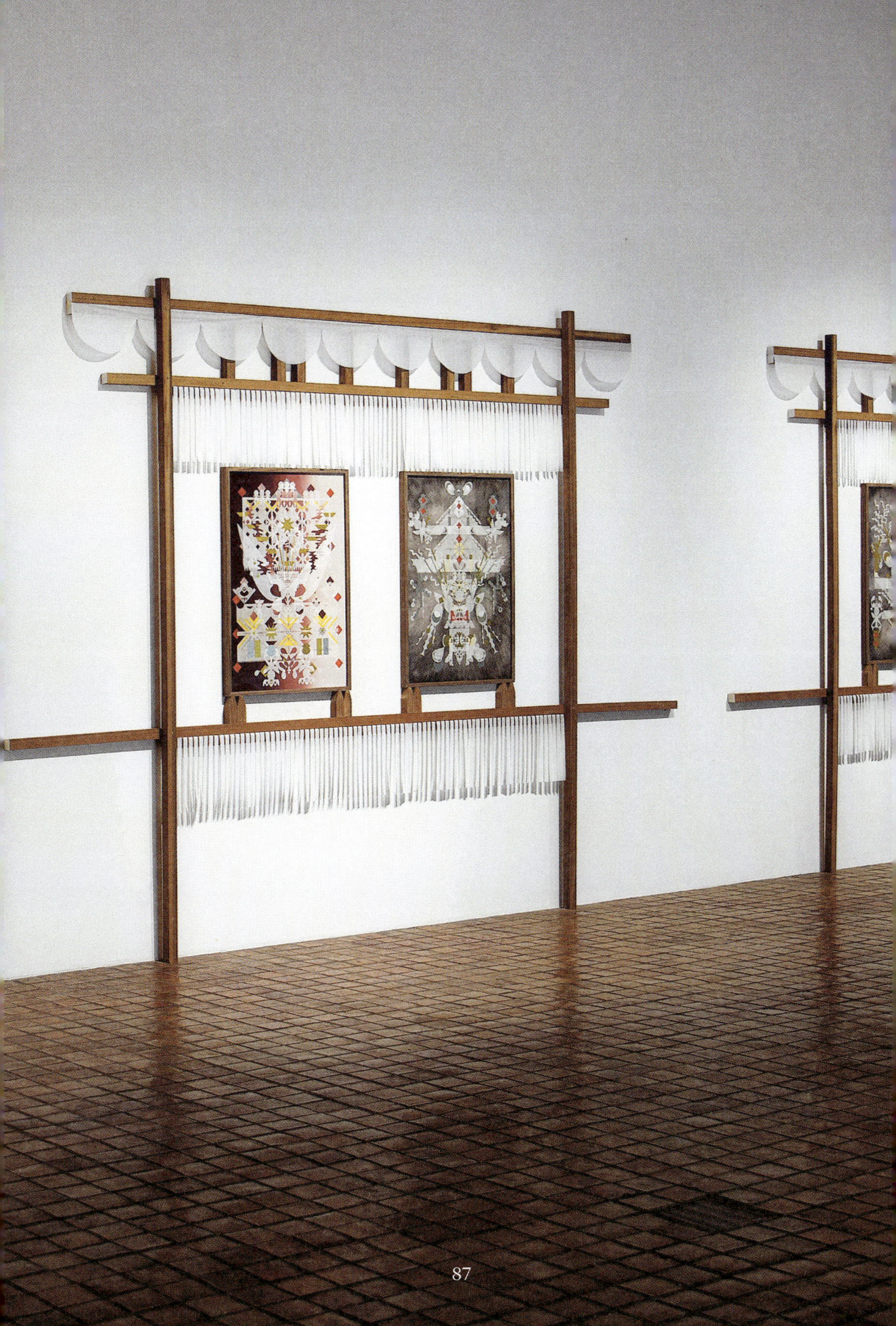

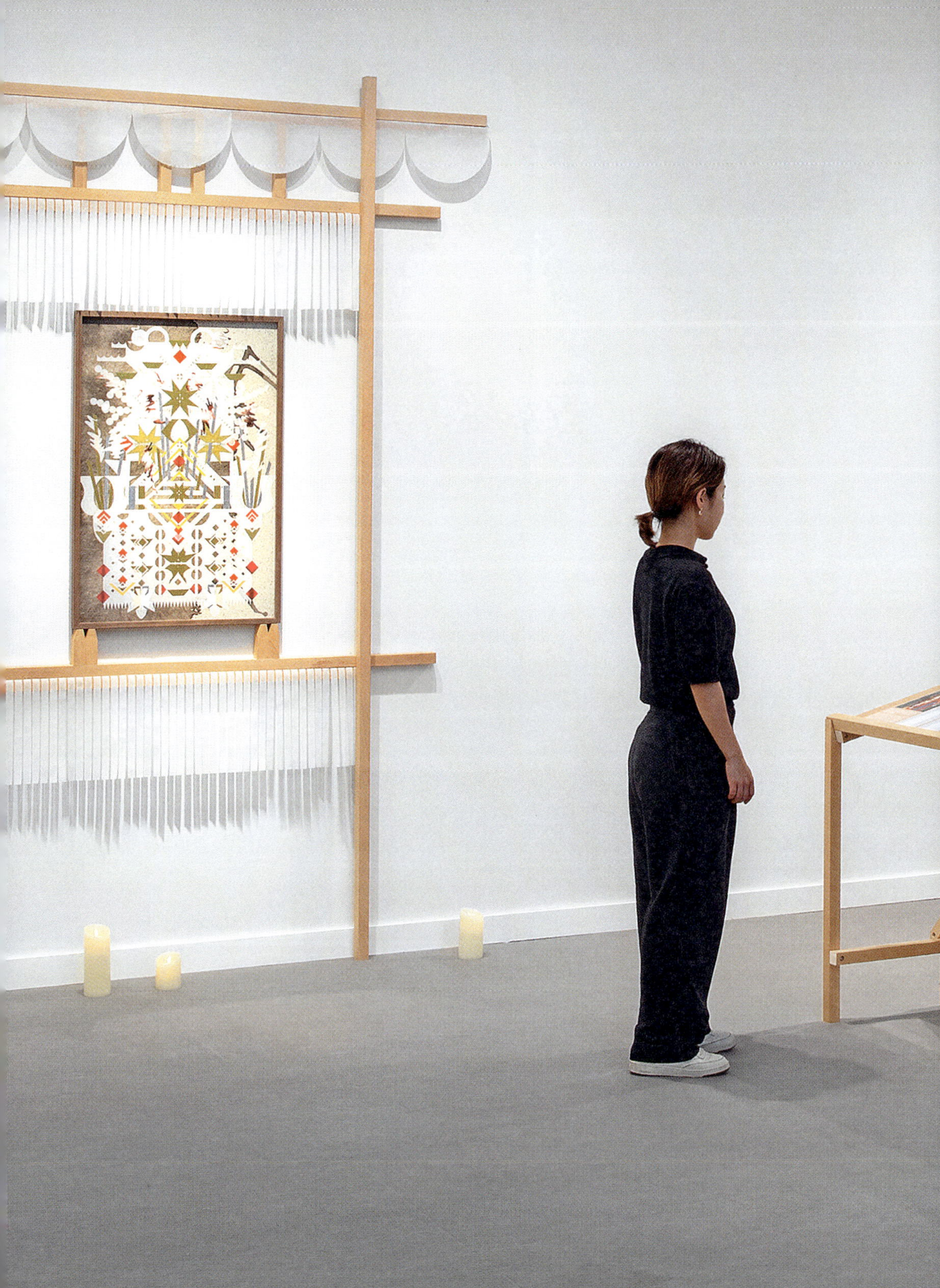

Kukje Gallery booth at Frieze New York, 2024

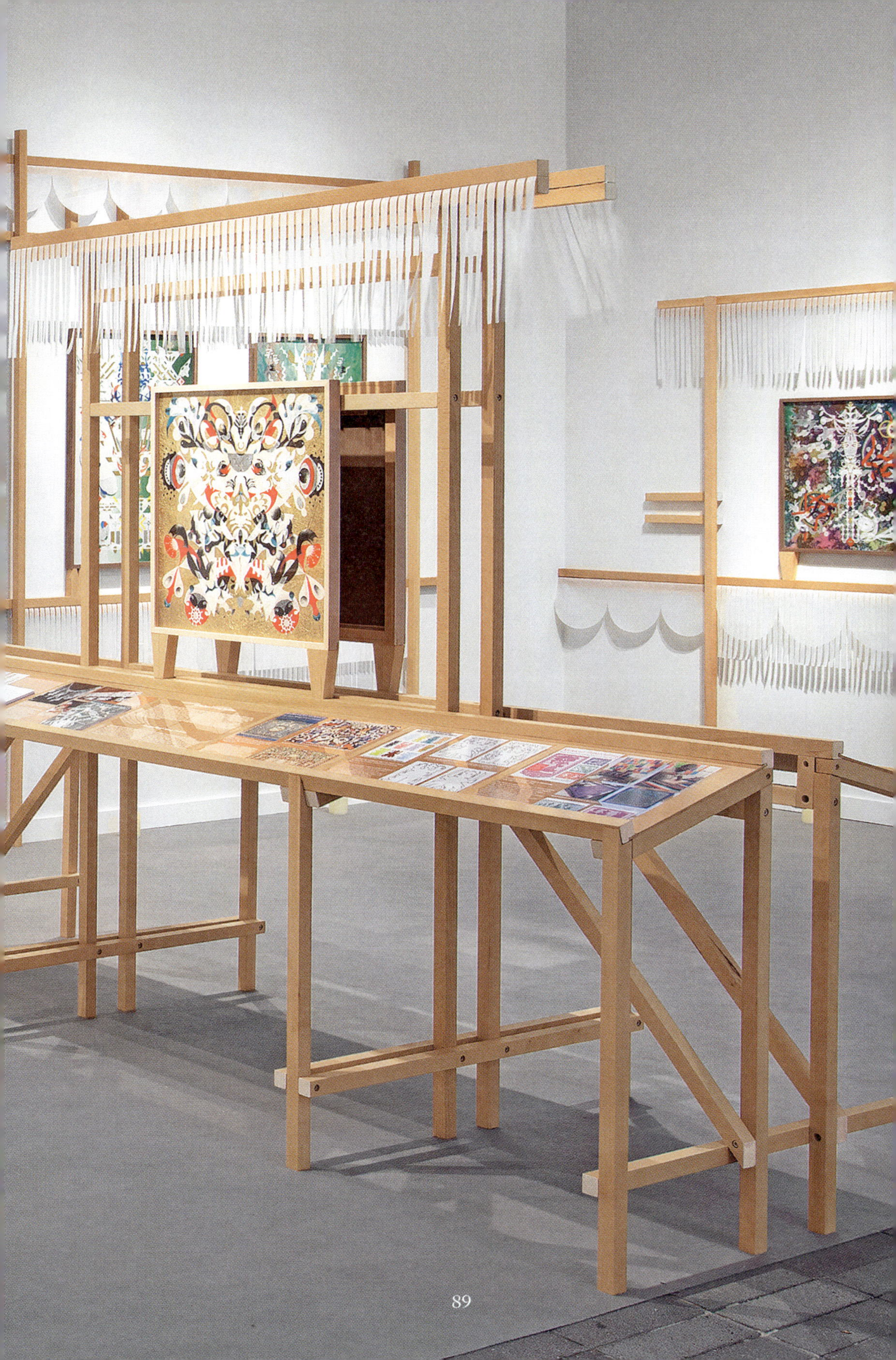

Illustrated Works

Pages

Curie, Saint-Cloud, France.
Photo: Jiayun Deng –
Galerie Chantal Crousel.

60 *Vegetable Print – Lotus
Pink #2* (detail), 2012
Relief print, embossing,
STPI handmade paper,
lotus root. 76.5 × 60.5 cm.
Produced at Singapore Tyler
Print Institute – Creative
Workshop & Gallery,
Singapore. Photo: STPI.

64 *Cinnamon Sheets Composition*,
2017. STPI handmade
mulberry paper, cinnamon
spices, framed. 5 parts, 78.5
× 78.5 cm each. Private
collection, USA. Installation
view of *Monochrome
Multitudes*, Smart Museum
of Art, The University
of Chicago, USA, 2022.
Photo: Tyler Mallory.

66 *Icy Mane Woven Soul Eyes –
Mesmerizing Mesh #236*
(detail), 2024. *Hanji, washi,*
origami paper on alu-
dibond, framed. 62 × 62 cm.

74 Installation view of *Haegue
Yang: Mesmerizing Mesh –
Paper Leap and Sonic
Guard*, Galerie Barbara
Wien, Berlin, Germany,
2022. Photo: Nick Ash.

76 *Gymnastics of the Foldables*
(detail), 2006. 15 b/w
photographs, framed
34.8 × 28.1 cm each.

80 *Imperfections*, 2010.
Installation view of
*Haegue Yang: Family of
Equivocations*, Aubette 1928
and Musée de Strasbourg,
France, 2013. Photo:
Mathieu Bertola, Musées
de la Ville de Strasbourg.

82 *Incantations – Entwinement,
Endurance, and Extinction*
(detail), 2022. Digital color
print on self-adhesive vinyl
film, paper pinwheels.
Dimensions variable.
Installation view of *Le Jardin:
incantation – incarnation*,
FRAC Champagne-
Ardenne, Reims, France,
2024.Photo: Aurélien Mole.

86 *Enveloped Domestic Soul
Channels – Mesmerizing
Mesh #208*, 2023. *Hanji,
washi*, origami paper on
alu-dibond, framed, shorea
wood, paint, wood stain.
6 parts, 62 × 62 cm; 92 ×
62 cm. Installation view of
The Open World, Thailand
Biennale 2023, Chiang
Rai, Thailand, 2023.

88 Installation view of
Kukje Gallery booth at
Frieze New York 2024.
Courtesy of Kukje Gallery.
Photo: Sebastiano
Pellion Di Persano.

This publication is
produced on the occasion of
Haegue Yang: Flat Works
The Arts Club of Chicago
September 18–
December 21, 2024

Curator
Janine Mileaf

Curatorial Assistant
Mia Morettini

Design
David Khan-Giordano

Studio Haegue Yang, Berlin
Liene Harms
Cheongjin Keem
Nicolas Pelzer
Marie Rime
Katharina Schwerendt
Emmy Skensved
Magnus von Ziegesar

Studio Haegue Yang, Seoul
Hwiwon Chun
Sangho Ha
Heeyun Im
Insun Kim
Julie Jeonghyen Kim
Myoungjung Kim
Seungnam Kim
Sihyun Ryu
Nayeon Sim
Solkyu Yang
Heejung Ye

First published in Italy in 2024
by Skira editore S.p.A.
Via Agnello 18
20121 Milano
Italy
skira-arte.com

Printed and bound in Italy.
First edition

ISBN: 978-88-572-5326-8

Distributed in USA, Canada,
Central & South America
by ARTBOOK | D.A.P.,
75 Broad Street, Suite 630,
New York, NY 10004, USA.
Distributed elsewhere in
the world by Thames and
Hudson Ltd., 181A High
Holborn, London WC1V
7QX, United Kingdom.